TRANSITION OR TRANSFORMATION?

also by John Clements

People with Autism Behaving Badly
Helping People with ASD Move On from Behavioral
and Emotional Challenges
ISBN 978 1 84310 765 1

Assessing Behaviors Regarded as Problematic for People
with Developmental Disabilities
John Clements and Neil Martin
ISBN 978 1 85302 998 1

Behavioural Concerns and Autistic Spectrum Disorders
Explanations and Strategies for Change
John Clements and Ewa Zarkowska
ISBN 978 1 85302 742 0

also by Stephanie Lord

Planning to Learn
Creating and Using a Personal Planner with Young People
on the Autism Spectrum
Keely Harper-Hill and Stephanie Lord
ISBN 978 1 84310 561 9

TRANSITION OR TRANSFORMATION?

Helping young people with Autistic Spectrum Disorder set out on a hopeful road towards their adult lives

John Clements, Julia Hardy and Stephanie Lord
with graphics support from Matt Whelan

Jessica Kingsley Publishers
London and Philadelphia

First published in 2010
by Jessica Kingsley Publishers
116 Pentonville Road
London N1 9JB, UK
and
400 Market Street, Suite 400
Philadelphia, PA 19106, USA

www.jkp.com

Library of Congress Cataloging in Publication Data
Clements, John, 1946 Dec. 1-
  Transition or transformation? : helping young people with autistic spectrum disorder
set out on a hopeful road towards their adult lives / John Clements, Julia Hardy and
Stephanie Lord.
     p. cm.
  ISBN 978-1-84310-964-8 (alk. paper)
  1. Autistic children--Education. 2. Autism spectrum disorders. 3. Autism--In
adulthood. I. Hardy, Julia. II. Lord, Stephanie. III. Title.
  LC4717.5.C54 2010
  371.94--dc22
                              2009051752

British Library Cataloguing in Publication Data
A CIP catalogue record for this book is available from the British Library

ISBN 978 1 84310 964 8

Printed and bound in Great Britain by

MPG Books Group, Cornwall

CONTENTS

ACKNOWLEDGEMENTS

We would like to thank all the staff, students and families we worked with over the time period covered by this book. Their ideas, challenges, encouragement and support all helped to shape the work described here. Three members of the senior management team deserve particular mention. Sarah Sherwood and Bryan Hynard played a huge role by turning training and ideas into effective practice. They played key leadership roles in creating exceptional teaching and learning experiences for our students. We did not always agree with each other, but through a shared commitment to teamwork we were always able to reach consensus. Keely Harper-Hill was the speech and language therapist for much of the time period in question. She was a major driving force behind many of the communication techniques described here and drafted the first BERIS manual. She was an effective and inspirational trainer – she would rehearse the senior management team until we were word, gesture and mantra perfect. She directly shaped our own presentation skills and was always there to model new practice ideas. We would also like to thank Laurence Hime, Principal Educational Psychologist, for the key role he played in building the skills of staff in the school, that for the purposes of this book we are referring to as Risinghill. We were fortunate indeed to have colleagues of this calibre.

A special thanks is due to Professor Phil Reed and his colleagues at Swansea University who took time out of a busy schedule to provide us (in Appendix 2) with a very thorough overview of their major research studies that included Risinghill.

We would also like to thank the team at Jessica Kingsley Publishers and Jessica herself in particular. She has been a source of great encouragement and gentle guidance in making sure this work came to publishable fruition.

Finally we would like to thank our families. Much writing goes on in 'stolen' time and can only be achieved with their forbearance. We thank them for that and for all the other things that they contribute make it possible for a project like this to be completed.

TRANSITION AND TRANSFORMATION

What is this book about?

This is a story of hope. The book describes an approach to working with a group of articulate adolescents on the autistic spectrum, a group who presented with highly significant behavioural challenges and emotional difficulties and who had been excluded from their previous educational placements. This work was carried out in a school setting specialised for students with autistic spectrum difficulties and illustrates how unpromising beginnings can turn into promising developments.

The book describes the support practices adopted at the school, practices that evolved over a number of years. It considers these practices in some detail and describes the outcomes achieved for the students both in terms of specific behavioural changes and more general changes in self-esteem and well-being. These changes are reflected in the kinds of opportunities that opened up for our students as they transitioned into early adult life; it is the contention of the book that these opportunities were much different to what might have been expected for such a disturbed group of young people.

However, the book goes beyond just enumerating specific practices. It locates these practices in a broader, systemic, whole school approach. In this way support practices for staff become as important as support practices for students. Education becomes a joint effort, a community of learning and development rather than something that educators do to students. The book illustrates how an initially small group of people shaped a climate and style of working that came to be adopted by the whole staff group and led to an organisation that as a whole was open, creative and solution focused. Thus attention is given in the text to key organisational characteristics and methods of organisational change because without such a holistic framework of support the individual practices with students become relatively meaningless.

Who are the authors?

The authors were involved in this work in varying ways. Stephanie Lord was the headteacher of the school in question and played the key leadership role in developing and sustaining the work described here. In many ways this book is a tribute to Stephanie's remarkable career and to her contribution in the field of autism. Julia Hardy was one of the educational psychologists for the school. She played a particularly important role in shaping up and sustaining the educational practice of staff and in fostering the creative 'can do' approach that came to typify the school organisation as a whole. John Clements was a clinical psychologist who played a much more intermittent role in staff training on behavioural issues and consulting about organisational development

Who is the book for?

This book is primarily for educators interested in the field of autistic spectrum disorders. It is for those who are directly involved in teaching students, for those who lead education services and for those concerned with the planning and management of educational services for this group. It provides both practical tips and broader based concepts that contribute to quality educational and life outcomes for our students.

However, we would also hope that the book is of some interest to parents. In the first place we would wish that the book provides families with hope for the future and grounds for optimism. For families dealing day in day out with long-term major behavioural challenges, coping with multiple and repeated school exclusions and the near absence of any meaningful family support services the future can come to look very bleak. Their present reality is tough indeed. We would wish that it were not so, but we would want to convey that there is hope, that despair is not the only option. However, optimism needs substance. We would also want the book to help parents think about the kinds of educational settings that would work best for their sons and daughters. We are firm believers in families having choices and reject the notion that one way works for all. However, to have meaningful choice families must know what to look for when they are evaluating an educational provision. We hope that by detailing the practices and philosophies that drove our approach it will help parents to think specifically about what sorts of education service would work best for their child so that they can know better what they are looking for.

Finally we hope the book will have some merit for a much smaller group – those who provide psychological services to people with ASD.

Recent developments in clinical psychology services have tilted these services towards providing 'therapy' for defined 'mental health' conditions. We see this shift as seriously mistaken. There may be a small role for 'therapy' but it is icing on the cake, not the cake itself. The cake is how we can work with living environments, particularly in this case, school and family, and intervene in these environments to generate supports that can be implemented consistently and persistently. It is everyday living environments that have the major influence over the thoughts, feelings and behaviours of individuals. It is the work of psychological services therefore to be involved in those environments to help generate the supports that will optimise the long-term outcomes for our students. This book is a powerful story in support of such a view and a counter weight to the view that psychology is to be equated with therapy.

How is the book organised?

The opening chapter provides background information on the school and the young people and presents the thoughts and ideas that drove the development of the service. The next two chapters are made up of vignettes describing some of our students and staff and the changes that took place for them over time. After a chapter detailing the view of autism that guided our thinking about supports, the next six chapters look in detail at specific approaches that were adopted and formed a long-term part of the work undertaken. There is then an attempt to evaluate the work and the impact it had upon the students' and staff's lives. The final chapter reviews the organisational supports that enabled the work to be done and then looks at what is involved in helping organisations to change. There are two Appendices: one an example of staff training materials and the other an extensive review of the research work undertaken by Professor Phil Reed and colleagues at Swansea University that illuminates some of the impacts of the school regime.

Chapter 1

THE BEGINNING

Introduction

A moment of crisis can be also an opportunity. In 2001, the local authority decided to close our special school as part of their policy on inclusion. The school was for children with autism, most of whom would be regarded now as 'classically autistic', with significant accompanying learning disabilities. The decision to close was not unexpected, but it coincided with the appointment of new members to the senior management team, who came together with a wealth of experience in the field of autism.

Faced with this challenge we became a committed team willing to develop new ideas in order to support the survival of the school. We had received a very good Ofsted (Schools Inspectorate) report and had a strong reputation for the development of the arts curriculum, especially massage, movement and drama. With the support of the governing body, we were able to seek independent status, and to offer our services to other local authorities. We will refer to our school as Risinghill.

This book will describe the functioning of the school between 2001 and 2006. Over this time the school increased in size from 20 up to 54 places. It was originally a mix of day and residential provision, but by the end of the period in question it was almost entirely a day school. Although the approach developed (and described in this book) was applied to all pupils at the school, the focus of this book will be a cohort of 18 students who joined the school in early adolescence and had moved on or were about to move on to the next stage in their lives by the end of the period in question.

Description of our 'new' students

Meetings with SEN (Special Educational Needs) Officers identified a group of secondary-aged students who had received a late diagnosis and were identified by the term autistic spectrum disorders (ASD). Among this group were children described as having high functioning autism or Asperger's syndrome and many had accompanying diagnoses including Tourette's syndrome, obsessive-compulsive disorder, attention deficit and hyperactivity disorder and mild psychosis. All of the children had expressive language, but their comprehension, understanding and interpretation of the school experience varied. Although perceived as academically able, in reality most children were functioning at a level significantly below their chronological age.

The majority of students in this first cohort of referrals had been excluded from school for a range of challenging behaviours. Most had been out of school for over a year. Those children still in full-time education received an allocation of tuition from a specialist teacher or a learning support assistant. A number of these children had attended or were attending anger management groups or social skills groups run by the education or health staff. A small cluster of verbal but passive non-communicative students were also referred to us.

In order to understand what was in part a new population of students for us we tried to observe them in their current school or unit setting, and with parental permission in their home environment. This group displayed very different behaviours from our previous experience of autism. Commonly these were children who appeared to engage in idiosyncratic behaviours regardless of the activity or setting going on around them. During this period we met children who appeared to spend the majority of their day wandering around school sites followed by a member of staff. We saw a lesson where one boy hid under the table, while another boy would not remove his coat and gloves and continually carried all his personal belongings in a big bag with him. Frequently we would see children seeking attention; shouting out was common as was taking offence at the behaviour of other children in the class.

Some students appeared disengaged from the reality of the classroom, staring at the ceiling or completing word search books for prolonged periods of time. Set work was rarely completed in the mainstream classroom, but finished in a quieter detached environment such as a smaller room or a special unit. These children seemed to prefer formal maths work, or work sheets where they could colour in, join dotted lines or fill in missing words. The common element would appear to be that these activities although not challenging, guaranteed a successful outcome. There was little or no age appropriate imaginative work and more complex written work was often completed with the help of a learning support assistant. It was quite usual to see an adult dictating words and sentences for a student to write.

In the home environment, it was clear that many family routines were dominated by these children. There were familiar themes such as control of the TV, the type of food eaten and the time meals were served. In one house mirrors were turned to face the wall. In another, old books, newspapers and magazines were stacked from floor to ceiling. There were also worrying examples of obsessions where a bedroom contained knives and an air gun, and another where a 12-year-old had a number of soft porn pin-up posters. Parents had become compliant in order to sustain peace and quiet at home.

Frequently children spent most of their time at home in their own room watching TV or playing on the computer while following their preoccupations. These ranged from simplistic cartoons being watched repeatedly, to 'sci-fi', violent or pornographic films. Where children were more social, family outings were controlled by their routine preference. These might include shopping in specific shops for individual items, for example Tesco for biscuits, ASDA for cereal and WH Smith for magazines, card or computer games. Activities would frequently be time-controlled by the child. Failure to meet time deadlines would cause disruption for the family. Conversely one or two children spent their days travelling on buses or trains, with or without a ticket, with no apparent time frame for when they should be home.

The parents told similar stories of struggling for many years with children who displayed a lack of emotional attachment to them. Emotional and behavioural outbursts, often linked with physical and verbal aggression were common. There were recurring health issues such as poor sleep patterns, toileting issues, faddy eating and lack of basic hygiene. Many children had been prescribed medication at some time for anxiety or mood disorders where extremes of temper were being shown.

Parents had received a range of professional support, but most parents reflected that they found the advice that they had received contradictory or conflicting. A familiar theme was that they believed that they had been advised to be more tolerant and accommodating to their child's need. The specific behaviours being displayed were explained as integral to the autistic condition. One mother described how her child's behaviour had been more acceptable when he was little, but now in adolescence appeared bizarre and he 'looked odd'. Parents were embarrassed and struggling to cope with a range of behaviours that were out of control. Some parents had attended counselling sessions with varying degrees of satisfaction. There were few examples of parents having seen professionals working directly with their child or having been shown how to put ideas into practice.

Overview of the challenges faced by these young people
Unaddressed learning disabilities

In a one-to-one situation, these children could appear relatively bright, capable of intelligent thought and discussion related to their topic of interest. Personal interests included insects, birds, chickens, cars, motor racing and the Beatles. Interests were expressed in a 'declamatory' way which often prevented a two-way conversation.

Educational testing had identified additional learning difficulties involving perception, visualisation, conceptualisation and coordination, but these had not been specifically addressed in the support offered. In the context of an academic subject-based curriculum, these students could be seen (and were often seen) as lazy, careless or clumsy.

Traumatised...but

For all the apparent bravado of some students, there was also significant vulnerability. A few children had been coerced or engaged in sexual behaviour such as mutual masturbation and oral sex. A couple of the older boys aged 12 and above were drinking excessively on a regular basis. All the children had been bullied at some time, experiencing name calling, having their possessions taken or being targeted for money. Actions against them often escalated over time into physical attacks. In one example a student had been set up to steal from a shop while other gang members waited outside.

Although vulnerable from one point of view, this group of children in their new school could also turn a classroom into an unsafe environment, making others vulnerable. They would express themselves in the form of sexualised language, knock over and throw chairs, throw books and equipment at staff and students, slam or kick doors. Thus they could traumatise others.

Lacking personal well-being

Our new students were not a happy group. Some children appeared pale and tired, and if a task required effort or energy they would attempt to avoid it. Problems with maintaining a focus or concentration were recurring issues. It was hard to find things that were pleasing or satisfying for them to do. Their attention style was a 'one go' approach, a 'don't like that – can't do it' attitude prevailed over the learning strategies that we had previously used with success. Their facial expressions were bland (when not anguished) and real enjoyment seemed hard for them to access.

Engagement in lessons where an authoritative teaching style prevailed would become a struggle to maintain control and direction. These children appeared to engage in activities where they were initiator and arbitrator, there seemed little acknowledgement that there could be a compromise.

Many seemed to be angered when attention was given to others in the group – this was often perceived as unfair ('unfair' being a very prominent way of viewing social situations). Operating at this emotionally fragile level meant that new situations were met with a primitive fight or flight response, possibly followed by a retreat to a preferred repetitive activity. The range of these activities included looking at a magazine or catalogue, drawing small circles, tearing strips of paper, stabbing a pencil into wood or soft material, etching their name on brickwork, digging a hole, or wandering around looking for adult support. Some would sit passively, seemingly divorced from events around them.

As familiarity in the new school environment developed, students began searching out senior staff or a favoured person. This had been a tried and tested technique used as a task avoidance strategy. To address this strategy we became firm and consistent in our approach. It was emphasised that all staff are here to help and mantras were developed, such as, 'How can I help you?' followed by, 'Let's check your timetable.' This often meant clarifying or writing down information for a student in order to resolve a situation that had previously occurred. Better understanding of the importance of hydration and nutrition meant that we might also offer a drink and a snack on the understanding that these would provide the energy for the student to get back on task. Taking a five-minute break was seen an acceptable activity. Opting out of education was not.

The start of the day was a particularly fragile time for the students. Arrival at school in the morning gave staff an indication of the children's mood or emotional state. Certain children would arrive looking tired and exhausted, stating that they had not eaten at home and requesting food. Some children arrived ready to enact a reprisal on a member of staff or student who had previously upset them. Others engaged in pacing or shouting in the playground. As arrival in school was an especially contentious time, it was necessary for staff to adopt a high level of alertness as students' behaviour could be extremely unpredictable. Meeting and welcoming children was a fundamental part of developing our helping response.

Throughout the day a significant number of children demonstrated a consistent pattern of withdrawal from classroom settings. For some wandering seemed important, others needed to check out what was happening in various areas of the school, some would withdraw to a seated area with their book or playing cards. At other times particular groups of students 'flocked' together, sharing an interest such as playing cards, but then quickly becoming argumentative with each other. The group could become aggressive towards a member of staff who tried to resolve issues.

Emotional breakdown was a frequent occurrence, with children showing a loss of control, crying and sobbing hysterically, or running away and damaging the environment. Once at a distance individuals would scream repeatedly, 'You don't understand,' 'You don't care' and 'It's not fair.' What they appeared to be communicating was an assessment of the situation that represented them as the victim of that situation.

One boy would conceal tablets and store them up, taking several at a time and subsequently becoming excited by the side effects. Another refused to take his medication which allowed his moods to fluctuate to the point where he spoke of harming himself or his father.

Lacking confidence

Motivation to learn was a major problem. With limited strategies children would retreat or move to impulsive outbursts as their only method of asking for help. Tasks that were not understood would be met with a negative response such as calling out 'rubbish', 'childish' or 'boring'. Children seemed unable to experience staff as helpful people and repeated patterns to elicit a negative response so that they could conclude (once again) 'You won't listen, you don't care.' A passive group would sit and continue with their personal interests and activities.

Despite the age and sometimes sophistication of the students, it became clear that they remained also at the stage of early sensory learning. The children needed to touch real materials and sharing was not an option; each person needed his/her own kit or resource box. When handling equipment each child showed a different response and it became possible to identify a dominant sense of touch, sight and sound. A few children still had a need to smell and taste. These combinations of maturities and immaturities represent a huge challenge to the process of education, particularly as the students get older.

First moves
Finding the purpose of education

The first year was a struggle. We modified the national curriculum but with limited success. These were secondary-aged boys, at one level very bright but who needed to operate with a very practical hands-on approach to learning. We also needed to address specific learning difficulties.

A small number of parents were dissatisfied with practical learning, but generally parents were supportive, turning up in good numbers for meetings and social events. At the end of the first year our annual report to parents was paired with a summer sharing and barbeque, thus ensuring a good turnout. Two parent governors led the discussion suggesting a change in our approach to the delivery of the curriculum.

Research from the NAS (National Autistic Society) identifying that less than 6 per cent of young adults with ASD gained open employment prompted our discussion. Those who did gain employment were involved in a supported living scheme or in a job where there was a family connection. This high rate of unemployment was a key focus for our concern about the kind of life that we should be preparing our young people for.

Parents were realistic in discussing their child's future; they expressed concerns about their child's behaviour and recognised that this could be a barrier to employment. Several things stood out at this meeting. Two members of staff, who were respected by parents, talked about their work. The chef talked about catering work and how he started as a dishwasher and gained National Vocational Qualifications (NVQs), the site manager explained that he had several college degrees but it was working practically, that gave him job satisfaction. A mother who was the Human Resource manager for a large company presented the view that employers were more 'disability aware' and would consider people who knew how to work and who could follow instructions. Parents explained that much of their own employment reflected a relatively non-social environment such as postman, milkman, labourer and decorator. This consensus shaped our governors' thinking and allowed us the confidence to formulate a curriculum linked to NVQs that we would describe as Education for Employability.

Developing the staff team

Auditing the skills of support staff produced a wide range of available skills – bricklayer, painter, engineer, athletics coach, a cyclist, an artist, a photographer, a florist and a Duke of Edinburgh Award leader. Volunteers added massage and yoga to the available skill sets. Roles were redefined so that staff's primary role was as job coach, work partner, life skill tutor or learning assistant. We attracted staff who had a desire to work with children, possessed the specific skill that could be used in our environment, but who did not have a formal teaching qualification. The potential for enriching the curriculum became enormous.

We worked with a special needs advisor and created a theoretical framework for our approach, utilising the available strengths and skills of the staff. Learning would take place under three broad headings:

- Well-being.
- Work skills.
- World knowledge.

Well-being addressed issues relating to personal development; work focused on skill development, problem solving and teamwork. Daily newspapers were purchased for each class and headline stories, pictures and news items gave a relevance to subjects of the national curriculum as world knowledge. A culture of learning for all staff became important. A style for working was starting to emerge as 'This is what we do and this is how we do it.'

Initially the qualified teachers needed additional training in order to utilise the available staff talent. The six class teachers became known as curriculum leaders and were in effect managers of teams of staff.

By generating savings we were able to purchase on a more regular basis the two consultants who had a major impact on our way of working. They developed our thinking towards a more systemic style. They challenged us to be creative – to develop strategies and techniques and to teach in a way that would maximise our students' potential. Supporting the development of the lead practitioners through training and coaching became essential for cohesive team development which in turn led to better outcomes for children.

Although passionate about what we did, we were being trained to be less emotional and judgemental in the way we worked with the children, preferring to look at the evidence. A significant catch phrase became 'Let the data do the talking.'

Evolving implications
Relationships for learning

In training we looked at and analysed teaching styles and the way that learning was presented (see Appendix 1 for an example of a staff training session). By staff actively participating in an activity such as swimming, staff could offer a high level of personal support, representing an early stage of development. We encouraged and developed a culture of cooperative working relationships. Students and staff would work together on learning experiences and solve problems together. We cast students in the role of team leaders giving them the 'mantle of the expert'. This meant that adults took part in all activities alongside students.

Both the first two authors trained the lead practitioner team in interpersonal skills. We learnt approaches that were relevant to both staff development and students' needs. Being a good listener was important as was phrasing key questions to find solutions to daily issues without becoming emotionally engaged. In order to do this consistently we created a script for working on problem solving. This included the key questions, 'Tell me about… Why do you think this happened?/What else could you do?' and emphasised the importance of feedback in helping others by framing key questions, 'What did you do well?/What prevented you from doing better?/Has this happened before?/What worked then?' This script would conclude in the formulation of a plan. 'Let's make a plan' became a key mantra for our work. Regular meetings and training sessions were woven into the timetable as a positive aspect to the work with children rather than as an interruption to the day.

Staff became more involved in solving problems and developing new ideas. New concepts were presented visually and displayed for all staff to view. Anyone could comment using post-its, indicating agreement, disagreement or the need to clarify a misunderstanding. Gaining consensus about a new approach ensured a higher level of success and staff conformity in using this approach.

Thus we moved away from traditional, didactic approaches to teaching based on a clear difference in status between 'teacher' and 'student'. Relationships were on a more equal footing, solving problems together. With this came a commitment to creativity, accepting that there was not a standard answer to all questions…but also there was no problem that could not be solved.

A culture of celebration and positive regard

By increasing the use of rewards and positive praise we believed that we could support our children to become successful and competent. Specific praise was used to identify for a student a significant stage of improvement, a task achieved or a correct decision made. Our approach needed to reflect to children a picture of themselves as thinkers and learners that would in consequence enhance self-esteem. We wanted them to feel empowered, effective decision makers and proud of their achievements.

However, such praise can only make an impact if there is a genuine appreciation of the student…and some students were hard to like. Training to look at unpleasant behaviours and finding an aspect of personality that could be viewed positively became of central importance. To work successfully with a student you needed to be able to like one thing about them and to recognise that this could be developed into a positive attribute. It took time to develop the confidence to admit that some staff might not like a student.

A culture of accountability

When behaviour broke down, children were acknowledged as being responsible for the choices that they made. Making a mistake or committing to a wrong choice was seen as an integral part of the developmental process. On the occasions when it was necessary to remove a student from a learning activity a consistent pattern was followed. Within a short period of time students accepted that going to a neutral environment was part of the process of acknowledging that something had gone wrong and that it was possible to repair situations with supportive adults. Developing an understanding that their thinking or actions had been inappropriate or misinterpreted and that it was possible to reach a positive solution, was seen as part of the pattern of daily living.

Creating the student handbook was a significant step forward in establishing expectations of behaviour that were to be followed by all children and implemented consistently by all staff. We were now prepared to explain social rules that had a consequence in the real world – for example that there were private words that could not be used at work, and that theft and aggression would be considered gross misconduct and had non-negotiable, identifiable sanctions attached.

Creating a supportive environment

As we increasingly understood the importance of creating a structure to our work, we also became committed to the creation of a nurturing environment. We understood that buildings and spaces could be stressful places. We regularly cleared clutter and organised materials for ease of access. Attention was given to the way work was labelled, mounted and displayed. Photographs of achievements were kept in albums or Life Journals as positive memories of achievement. Lead practitioners were vigilant in walking the building on a daily basis, checking the relevance of displays and improving an area that could be confusing for students.

Research on brain development led us to understand the importance of fresh air and exercise. Time for walking and thinking were built into the programmes. We made seating and rainproof areas that we called safe havens where students were allowed to go without staff interference or intrusion on the understanding that staff, as carers, would always observe from a distance. Plants and flowers became important and we accepted the theory that plants improved the atmosphere in the day time and oxygenated the environment. They also lifted our spirits!

The alignment of staff management practices

It was understood that moving towards this way of working with our students had profound implications for staff management. You could not create a collaborative problem-solving approach with students and use authoritarian approaches to manage staff. The collaborative approach had to pervade the entire system and all staff had to feel empowered. This was achieved in a number of ways – redefining roles, full participation in decision making, the active encouragement of new ideas and questioning practice, training, 'managers' working side by side and hands-on with 'staff' and everyone developing their interpersonal skills such as listening, asserting and speaking honestly. Although this kind of approach attracts current attention with terms such as 'distributed leadership', our own understanding dates from much earlier ideas that were developed in the 1970s about how to manage systems to get good outcomes when working with people regarded as challenged and challenging (e.g. Clements 1987, Chapter 8 in this book).

Concluding remarks

It took three years to create the model that is described in this book. It developed over time as our understanding of our students and of what we were trying to do evolved. It did not happen all in one go. We did reach a point of having a 'house style' but this was nurtured and refined on a constant basis – the learning and, we hope, the improvement continued.

Out of this work emerged a very large number of specific techniques that we found helpful to our students. Much of the book is given over to describing these techniques. However, we hope it has been clear from this first chapter that this was a very significant journey for both our students and our staff. The next two chapters will look at these journeys for some of the individuals involved, to give a more personal feel for what the work was about.

Chapter 2

STUDENT STORIES

This chapter will describe five individual students, their history and their educational journey during their time at Risinghill. For each individual we will try to bring alive for the reader how each young person changed their thinking, attitudes and behaviour during the time at Risinghill and where they headed, or intended to head, next on their journey. The stories are based on personal reminiscences and interviews with the student. The students gave their permission for the information to be used in this way.

Ben
Diagnosis and early history
Ben, who was diagnosed with Asperger's syndrome at 14, had difficulties of social interaction and communication, showed evidence of obsessions and needed to follow rules and routines. He was very literal in his understanding and had low self-esteem. At the time of diagnosis Ben's conceptual ability was described as in the very low range.

His mother recognised that Ben was different as a baby. She described him as quiet and content to be by himself – 'he liked to bang his head on a chair'. He spent his early years in the garden, being with the dogs, feeding the chickens, looking after horses, going out with his grandfather. At nursery school Ben was identified as a loner – he would sit and day dream and not join in with the other children. Despite the very late diagnosis, Ben's behaviour shows from the early years difficulties that are consistent with the characteristics of autism.

It seems that significant problems for Ben started at infant school where he became more stubborn and found it hard to get on with other children. As he got older he became aggressive at home and would argue with his mother and sister, but not his grandfather. He collected cameras and mobile phones and liked to line up farm animals. If his mother moved them he would flail his arms around and bang his head on the wall. He would repeatedly watch his favourite video, 'The Ring of Bright Water'.

At nine years old Ben was described as bizarre and his problems identified as emotional and behavioural, and by ten he was given a specialist behaviour teacher. Staff recognised that he had particular difficulties with the identification of and application of rules that govern abstract relationships. It is interesting how the label EBD (emotional and behavioural difficulties) had been given to Ben, which made it difficult for staff to understand the implications of his behaviour that were in fact due to the complexity of his autism.

Although Ben was identified as a loner at nursery school it was not until his first term at secondary school that things came to a head and he was excluded for:

- punching a boy
- threatening a member of staff
- firing a catapult
- threatening a boy with a knife
- assaulting two teachers and having to be held
- uncontrollable rages.

There were a plethora of exclusions and in the end Ben was permanently excluded for attacking two pupils on a bus with a knife. He was then out of school for over a year before his placement at Risinghill.

Although the above includes descriptions of behaviour, there was a tendency for Ben to be portrayed as a deviant. We remember comments from previous schools such as his physical assaults having 'premeditation' about them; and in the same vein telling lies became 'pathological lying'. With hindsight we can see the long-term difficulties that Ben had experienced in making social relationships and understanding the consequences of his behaviours; and now see that reflected his autism rather than character defects.

Strengths and areas for improvement
Although there were on record a lot of negative evaluations of Ben there were also positive themes. He was said to:

- respond to careful and consistent support, but admitted that he did not like all staff, especially support assistants who moaned at him
- love animals and liked to talk about his dogs, chickens and his mum's horses
- like practical tasks and to prefer to work outside

- like to talk to his mum and sit with her, but she found this irritating when she wanted to watch the television.

There were also more specific difficulties itemised:

- Getting to the lesson on time.
- Bringing the right equipment.
- Not staying on task.
- Becoming distracted.
- Not presenting his work in a neat and tidy fashion.

However, the way that Ben was viewed made it hard to develop any constructive response to these difficulties at school.

How others viewed Ben
In addition to the deviant portrayal above, we recall a range of other negative comments made about him:

- At primary school an experienced headteacher 'kept an eye on him' when things got difficult.
- His specialist support teacher described him as being aggressive, bizarre and disruptive. He was said to have the ability to sabotage lessons with unnecessary comments.
- He was described at secondary school as attention seeking and disruptive.
- It was said that Ben had let himself down and let his attitude get in the way of his learning, that he should make more of an effort to fit in.
- When work was too difficult he was said to become impulsive and to lose self-control.

It appears that many school staff used unhelpful, generalised, labelling comments about Ben rather than recognising the fundamental issue of Ben's need for a structured environment to help him cope with the more specific difficulties outlined above. When his difficulties are understood as reflecting some of his basic needs they immediately become accessible to positive work, something not possible when they are viewed as generalised personal defects.

Managing emotions

Despite the difficulties Ben was described as very personable in a one-to-one situation with a trusted adult. However, he had unexplained sudden rages and used physical and verbal aggression towards his peers and teachers, with the adults interpreting this as Ben objecting to them challenging his authority.

At times Ben was described as becoming sad and morose. He knew that he had problems with making and keeping friends. He was aware that some friendships had led him into trouble and that he had been used by other students. He was aware of some of his difficulties and in an interview aged 11 identified that he needed 'help with behaviour', but when asked what type of help said, 'I don't know.' His mother reported that at home he cried and asked what was wrong with him. He said that the teachers would not listen.

Again, with hindsight it is possible to see these difficulties as reflecting Ben's autism – the difficulty with social rules and relationships, the difficulty of reflecting on and managing his own emotions, the vulnerability to loss of well-being in the face of life's challenges.

Transition and transformation at Risinghill

When Ben first started at Risinghill many staff questioned the appropriateness of his placement. Although he had recently been diagnosed with Asperger's syndrome, he was at first perceived as different and dangerous, and more inexperienced staff found it very difficult to work with his challenges. On one occasion the police were called when he threatened to hit the headteacher with a chair. There was a danger of history repeating itself.

Transformation through building a working relationship

Many things were put in place to avoid this outcome. One of the transformations for Ben occurred when it became apparent that he needed a specialist, skilled member of staff working as his dedicated key-worker. In discussions with senior staff he stated, 'It makes me feel special when someone talks about my dog – it is like they like me and not just my dog.' It was very evident that Ben loved animals. He also loved to be read to, and brought books on gun dogs and chickens into school. These features became the building blocks for more positive relationships. He took these books to the headteacher or senior staff and would sit looking intently as information was read to him from a manual on keeping hens, as if this was a story book. Over time it became apparent that such activities were crucial as building blocks to developing relationships with significant staff.

Transformation through personalisation

By the second term of Ben's placement the focus had changed to working with his strengths and personalising the approach to meet his needs and style. The strategy shifted from getting Ben functioning in a social group to planning motivating activities related to functional tasks. He was given the title of 'apprentice site assistant' working on maintenance projects with site staff. These included:

- Building a new chicken run.
- Sorting out equipment and being allowed to keep discarded items.
- Introducing literacy and numeracy concepts through task instruction sheets (see Chapters 5 and 7) that required a cross through or a tick box response.
- Being given a budget to calculate the cost of materials for specific projects.

These initial moves set in motion a positive sequence of events, leading to an outcome not predicted from Ben's early history.

Transition to adulthood

Ben left Risinghill and went to college. He qualified with Level 1 certificates from college having studied game-keeping and animal husbandry. He now works as a freelance handyman and wants to go back to college so he can find a better job. He particularly identified massage as being an important feature of the school regime, that helped him become more relaxed, calmer and more aware of himself.

Alan

Diagnosis and early history

Alan was first diagnosed with ASD at 15 years of age. He was seen as 'different from others' with low self-esteem and significant emotional distress. At this point he weighed 16 stone and was said to be developing an eating disorder. The one ray of hope was that he was seen as a child who responded well to positive encouragement.

Alan's mother described Alan as a passive baby and this theme carries through into descriptions of him at primary and secondary school. Alan babbled and pointed to things of interest, but was late developing words for objects. By the age of three Alan preferred to be by himself, playing with a dumper truck and ignoring Lego or other toys. Alan developed an issue with labels in clothing and his mum had to remove all the instruction tags before he would wear a garment. He disliked certain shoes.

At primary school Alan was seen as a fiddler and day dreamer. At eight years his mother was told that Alan was about two years behind his peers, but by ten he is described as five years behind. At this stage Alan received one hour a week additional support. He was said to use illness to escape from the classroom; although from another point of view he could be seen as showing signs of stress in lessons that he could not understand.

In secondary school, Alan was identified as a slow learner with specific problems, possibly dyslexia. He was given yellow tinted glasses and attended a literacy group. When Alan stopped doing his homework he was sent to a homework club, but this did not help with his learning difficulties.

Terms that we remember being used about Alan were 'reserved and anxious', 'needing support and encouragement', but these understandings did not seem to be translated into practical interventions at school. His opting out at school was seen as an issue of motivation linked to low self-esteem, but again this did not lead to any specific help.

At secondary school Alan was sent to specialist classes but he became school phobic and refused to attend school after being bullied in the toilets.

As a part of an assessment Alan remembered a meeting with a psychologist at which he made three wishes:

1. For the bullying to stop.

2. To get better at maths.

3. To be able to work with his hands at craft or something similar.

Strengths and areas for improvement
Three particular strengths for Alan had been flagged up:

1. He had a specific interest in mechanical areas.

2. He responded well to praise and encouragement.

3. He liked working with older students.

On the other hand there were a lot of difficulties identified:

- Below average IQ, with a literal mode of thinking.

- Poor memory and weak auditory sequencing skills.

- Poor relationships with his peers. He had never had a real friend, even at primary school, because he was unable to interpret the behaviour of others.

- Provoked arguments to gain the teacher's attention and became angry if his point of view was not heard or understood.

How others viewed Alan

Alan's story differs from Ben's in that he did come to the attention of teachers and the negative stereotypes generated were not so overpowering. However, because of his passivity and communication difficulties the attention he got did not lead to any real success from a constructive point of view. Rather it led to a different set of 'blame' statements, with him being described as lazy and passive, unwilling to engage in learning. So although the language differs from that applied to Ben, one can see again how describing the issues as personal, almost moral, defects interferes with any attempt to develop constructive support.

Managing emotions

Both his primary and secondary school realised that Alan liked routines and needed to know exactly what was happening. Timetable changes, for example, would cause anxiety and distress. He used to get cross over small incidents and would become verbally aggressive. Alan recalled that he found it hard to read people's faces and to know what they were thinking. He knew that it was wrong to hit people but was so overwhelmed by anger that he felt he had to 'storm around'. Alan was seriously bullied from the age of eight because of his slowness and size. He was not chosen for class teams or PE activities and was not liked. Alan expressed the view that staff did not like him or listen to him when he tried to tell them about other pupils pushing his head down the toilet and flushing it. After these traumatic experiences Alan refused to attend school.

Transition and transformation at Risinghill

Alan settled in easily to Risinghill and was pleased that people recognised his difficulties. Relationships developed as part of the ongoing work rather than requiring specific attention (as was needed for Ben). As time went on eating became less of an issue for Alan and the school approach to healthy eating immediately helped him.

Transformation through personalisation

At interview Alan identified that he wanted to be a mechanic. He said that cars and engines made sense to him and that he liked working on something that he completed and that was all his own work. With this information Risinghill personalised the approach for Alan by giving him opportunities to undertake activities with machines and do outdoor tasks involving tools and walking across the site to deliver messages. These experiences were then built upon by organising a period of work experience in a local garage.

Transition to adulthood

Alan left school at 18 to go and work in full-time employment in the local garage. During the first six months Alan repeatedly returned to school on a daily basis at lunch break to see one particular member of staff or to request a massage. Gradually Alan gained the confidence to stay at the garage throughout the whole day. Two years later Alan is still employed and has been accepted as an apprentice mechanic; he has passed his driving test and booked a holiday to Spain. His weight has now reduced to 11 stone.

Colin

Diagnosis and early history

Colin was diagnosed with EBD at an early age and was described as difficult to manage at his nursery school. Even at this stage he was seen as impulsive and restless, with behaviours such as running away and hiding.

Colin's behaviour at home led to admission to a residential primary school for children with EBD. Colin's mother stated that Colin 'found it impossible to keep quiet'. The behaviours that his mother found difficult to manage were:

- Making erratic and loud noises.
- Acting inappropriately in social situations, such as burping while eating.
- Self-harming with wire or screws.
- Damaging household property – scratching furniture.

She noted that he displayed these behaviours if he failed to get his own way.

Colin was eventually diagnosed with ASD at ten years of age, when his EBD school staff expressed their concerns that he was becoming increasingly vulnerable because of his 'bizarre' imagination and outbursts of uncontrollable laughter that verged on hysteria. Eventually Colin's behaviour intensified into more severe aggressive flare-ups and abusive language. This led to Colin physically attacking members of staff (kicking, spitting) and, on several occasions, trying to strangle female staff.

Colin's mother recalled that from quite early on Colin would 'play' fight with his younger brother. The fighting would consistently get out of control as Colin attacked him with a perceived intention to hurt. It is interesting that such intense physical acts that were prevalent in his early behaviour in the home are paralleled later in his behaviour at school. Colin still finds the concepts of reality and fiction difficult to separate and will state that he believes fictional TV programmes to be 'real'.

Strengths and areas for improvement

From early on Colin was noted as having severe or moderate learning difficulties. It was also noted that his receptive language was stronger than his expressive language. He was seen as someone who was slow at thinking and slow at moving. Later a diagnosis of dyspraxia was made and a series of exercises prescribed to address low muscle tone. It was obvious that Colin's needs were viewed in a number of contrasting ways by the professionals involved with him.

The stated view of his problems included:

- Problems with remembering and processing instructions.

- Delayed social interaction and inability to initiate interaction without aggression.

- Difficulties with gross motor actions – low muscle tone.

- Limited ability to make choices.

Managing emotions

Reports identified that from an early age Colin needed plenty of time for planning, preparation and assimilation. He was hard to move on from a chosen activity, whether this was appropriate or not. When not given sufficient processing time Colin would become abusive or aggressive to the adult, even if this adult was attempting to offer support. Colin showed obsessive mannerisms when out of control, such as flapping paper continuously and then chewing or tearing it when asked to give it back. When he threatened to break a window, Colin could not be diverted until he heard the sound of breaking glass. Increasingly there was concern noted about general safety around Colin. It was recommended that he should be supported at all times when working with peers, in order not to compromise their safety during a potential outburst. This is clear evidence of the intensity of Colin's outbursts.

Transition and transformation at Risinghill

The transition to Risinghill was difficult. Colin felt rejected and regarded a renewed residential situation a personal punishment. He often cried that he wanted to be at home with his parents and brother. Attacks on adults continued with equal intensity to those he had previously shown. He continued to target female members of staff, using his hands to grip at their necks. He threatened to kick a teacher and as she was leaving the room to get assistance he kicked her in the back, knocking her to the floor.

Colin would attempt to engage male teachers in 'combat games' and would find pieces of wood to use as weapons. When this strategy was nullified by staff agreement, Colin would attempt to find agency or site staff who might be more easily persuaded.

Colin's parents requested a referral to a 52-week residential school placement and the Child and Adolescent Mental Health Services (CAMHS) team became involved. He was referred to a psychiatrist who diagnosed ADHD as a co-morbid condition and prescribed Ritalin. From staff perspectives the medication seemed to make a difference and Colin became more 'manageable'. Colin himself also believed that his medication helped to calm him down.

Transformation through emotional management

The psychiatrist suggested a very direct warning system should be used with a consequence of a community sanction. Staff learnt to use a strategy of three warnings, which consisted of a graphic strip with three large items of information:

1. You need your sensible head – you need to calm down.

2. How can I help you to think/calm down?

3. You need to go to the function room to talk to xxxx.

The breathe and blow strategy (see Chapter 9) was particularly successful in helping Colin to control his breathing to calm down. At a later stage Colin was able to identify and use a 'safe haven' where he would go and sit and practise his breathing by himself. When Colin was not able to recognise the intensity of a situation for himself, staff used a 'take a break' card for five minutes time away in a quiet place. Later Colin realised that walking and 'dreaming' (as he described it) was calming and this was agreed with distanced supervision.

Transformation through personalisation

Colin liked the concept of 'silly head/sensible head' and used the term 'fuzzy' to describe times when he felt confused. Staff used these words as a thinking tool when Colin needed help. He used his 'I need help' card and found satisfaction in asking adults for help in a positive way and getting acknowledgement and assistance without causing a disturbance.

Improvements in self-esteem were noticeable and Colin started to repeat mantras that staff used to him such as 'I feel proud', 'I feel proud when I...' At 15, a significant breakthrough occurred when Colin indicated that he was beginning to notice personal physical and emotional changes around the trigger points. For instance, when given the important job of taking the orders for lunch from a group of adults he would prepare himself by deep calm breathing before undertaking the task. Colin used the 'happy hands' approach, using a hand on his chest to monitor breath control and a hand on his head to indicate when the 'fuzzy' feeling had passed. He could also sit with his hands in his lap for relaxation.

Colin started to enjoy using a new organiser which was reduced to a more sophisticated A5 Filofax format. He began to carry his 'I need help' graphic on a key ring. Reward points became important and he would work towards a long-term reward. He wanted to get extra reward points for massage sessions, as well as using his 'I need a massage' card on a daily basis. Colin identified that a back massage made him feel good.

Transition to adulthood

Colin is keen to go to a local college. He knows he will need help and talks about having an adult 'work assistant'. He likes maintenance and cleaning tasks and appreciates when things are clean and tidy. Colin refers to his task instruction sheet and uses a desk filing system for jobs – 'Just like I will do at work.'

Dean

Diagnosis and early history

Dean was diagnosed with Asperger's syndrome at the age of eight. It was apparent to his primary school teachers that he was unable to cope with the changes of routine that are common in daily school life. Dean was transferred to a unit for children with ASD that was part of a local primary school and he was educated there from the age of eight up to eleven. In the unit Dean was noted for his tendency to feel unwell, allied to a genuine asthmatic state. He was commonly described as a 'fragile' or 'delicate' pupil who preferred his own company. Not surprisingly Dean had few friends.

Presumably as a euphemism for appearing clumsy, Dean was described as having poor body awareness and was prone to spilling liquids and walking into furniture and doors. Dean would take a considerable time to get dressed, giving care to his presentation by patting or smoothing his clothing. In class he would similarly take a long time to organise his work and resources, and consequently had little time to complete tasks. He was remembered as a disorganised little boy with no friends.

The reports from nursery and primary school identify a passive child, who was content to be by himself and seemed to be self-absorbed, often staring into space and daydreaming. There were reports of sudden outbursts of temper, barging and charging, but these were unexplained and no specific antecedent was identified.

There was a different picture at home. Dean's parents stated that Dean was a difficult child who attempted to dominate the family, insisting on eating at a certain time, watching television programmes at a certain time and refusing to comply with reasonable requests. He would shout at his sister and father and retreat to his bedroom if he did not get his own way. At home it would seem that Dean tried to create his perfect world that did not involve changes to his routine.

Dean was also described as being 'aggressive' when playing with his younger sister. The nature of this play seemed to involve the difficulty that Dean had in separating fantasy from reality. The play fights with his sister would centre on a scenario constructed from Dean's favourite computer game. Although school was reporting that Dean had outbursts, at no stage is there any suggestion of intentional aggression towards another individual, adult or peer.

Strengths and areas for improvement

Dean's compliance was identified as his greatest asset. Language and communication were seen as his greatest problems, including:

- The limited use of pragmatic language.

- Mechanical reading.

- A lack of comprehension.

- Mechanical competency at spelling.

Dean's attempts to socialise were seen as immature and poorly developed, with an absence of eye contact and a stiff body posture. It was suggested that he should be referred to an occupational therapist for assessment, but no action appears to have been taken on this.

Managing emotions

The passivity that had been acknowledged at primary school continued in Dean's first year at Risinghill. This characteristic held up even in what would appear very difficult circumstances, for example he was unable to express sadness when his guinea pig died. He continued to enjoy his own company. Interestingly these attitudes intensified, in that he chose not to speak to the two girls in his classroom who found him attractive and wanted to talk to him.

As Dean was required to participate in a broader, more challenging curriculum that involved moving around the campus, it was noticeable that incidents of 'storming off' and 'verbal aggression' became more intense. When left alone Dean would appear vacant and not engaged, but clearly became anxious as demands were made of him.

Transition and transformation at Risinghill

The transformation for Dean came at a later stage. When the organiser system was introduced he immediately enjoyed using this to keep a record of his daily activities. He also used it to record a more personal account of his memory. When asked about something that had happened previously, Dean would look this up and say, 'Ah yes, now I remember.'

Transformation through motivational enhancement and communication accommodations

It became apparent to staff that as Dean was moving through adolescence his strategies of passive non-engagement were in themselves a hindrance to his learning. Two things occurred that gave staff a clue as how to progress with Dean. Reward sampling seems to have motivated him and he would always choose something to work towards. He also enjoyed earning reward points, physically recording these in his organiser three or four times a day. Staff could challenge his lethargic responses by offering a 'fast reward' (meaning an immediate one as soon as the task was completed) to get a job done.

The absence of pragmatic language identified in primary school was specifically addressed with scripted notes or task instruction sheets for Dean to use, which overcame his difficulties in understanding spoken language alone. These were filed in a desk-top filing system and he could refer to these as an aide-mémoire. Staff agreed that consistent and enthusiastic verbal praise would be given to Dean's use of agreed, scripted speech. Set phrases were agreed with Dean when rehearsing what he would need to say when communicating with others in functional tasks. This was also supported by the use of a reassuring touch to his arm or back in a 'well done' gesture. This positive touch seems to have contributed to his sense of well-being, as Dean is noted to 'have grown with positive praise'.

The use of video provided another breakthrough. While watching a film of himself carrying out office tasks, Dean noticed that he was having difficulty taking a telephone message. He thought he needed to be able to write faster and so staff were able to teach him speed writing, because his level of motivation to do this was so apparent.

Transformation through personalisation

At this time a group of young people from the local secondary school started visiting to take part in a 'buddy' project. Dean surprised staff by identifying that he would like to have a girl friend. A process of peer modelling took place as Dean took notice of hair styles. He started to come to school with his hair thick with gel and staff needed to show him how to gel his hair into shape without using a full tub!

At 16 Dean moved into a newly created group at school called the Apprentices. This involved undertaking a number of NVQ (National Vocational Qualification) courses that required changes in uniform for specific tasks. Dean enjoyed wearing a yellow T-shirt for cleaning tasks, but was especially taken with wearing a shirt and tie for business studies. We see the previous behaviour of attention to dress now having an appropriate response. He would smile when greeting staff and repeat the learnt mantra, 'It's important to present a professional image.'

At 18 Dean uses his organiser as a thinking tool. He has a special section to help him make plans for calming in response to anxious moments. He has created his own painting using blue and green colours for calm visualisation. He can be heard to quietly mutter 'breathe and blow' under his breath. Dean has also learnt to use a graphic, which he carries in his pocket: 'Count to ten and ask for help.' He has another graphic 'I don't understand – can you write it down?' on a Velcro strip on the front of his organiser which he transfers to a clip board when he has tasks to complete.

When working, Dean uses a green sticker to indicate any changes to his day and can use these with a learnt phrase 'OK, let's get this sorted.' He makes a joke of a confusing moment by saying, 'What was that again?' and rubs his palms together to give himself thinking time. Dean still enjoys a back massage and says it helps to calm him down.

Transition to adulthood
Dean has a worker who takes him out on a Saturday to the shops, where he is able to link up with a group of other people with special needs. He is not concerned about being identified as autistic as he thinks this helps people understand why he has problems. Dean is starting a basic skills course at his local college.

Ethan
Diagnosis and early history
Ethan attended mainstream primary school and seems to have made satisfactory progress reaching Level 3–4 at Key Stage 2. However, at the end of Year 1 in secondary school Ethan developed epilepsy and was diagnosed with a brain abnormality and subsequently with ASD. It was noted that Ethan's behaviour altered considerably and the epilepsy was described as having a significant impact on his ability to concentrate and to control impulsive behaviours. He was seen as having particular difficulties with concentrating when in large group situations and as becoming more behaviourally challenging. Outbursts were most likely in corridors and in the playground where the noise, lack of structure and number of students became a possible trigger to unacceptable behaviour. Incidents began to increase in severity with reports of physical aggression (lashing out) towards teachers and peers. By this time Ethan was starting to be described as showing uncontrolled anger and violent outbursts that threatened the safety of others. He was excluded from school on grounds of safety.

Although school associated the dramatic change of behaviour with Ethan's medical condition, Ethan's mother had been concerned long before this. She described him as 'always showing a level of difficulty in social situations'. She believed that in stressful situations Ethan's high level of anxiety made it difficult for him to communicate successfully. Ethan's mother described his behaviour as unusual and odd. Ethan found it difficult to assess how to behave appropriately in different situations. He would tell jokes that were inappropriate for the given audience, telling the same joke to his grandparents as he would to his school peers. He was not aware of his grandfather's look of shock when hearing swearing in the joke. Responding to social situations would lead to awkward moments such as smiling and laughing when someone had hurt himself.

These inappropriate responses at school led to misunderstanding and misinterpretation. So while Ethan is described as a friendly young man it is also noted that his engaging smile irritated people (for example, he was seen as 'smirking' when being told off).

Ethan's father saw his son's behaviour as similar to his own. He felt that they shared the same characteristics of being 'basically happy and easy going, but a bit forgetful'.

Strengths and areas for improvement

At the time of referral to Risinghill Ethan was described as:

- a friendly young man

- having an above average understanding of numeracy

- needing to improve in literacy.

But there were long-term themes relating to delayed social behaviour:

- He was immature for his age.

- He had poor social interaction with peers and adults.

- He sulked and frequently refused to work.

- He needed to learn social skills in order to be alongside others.

Difficulty in motor coordination was commented on more frequently after his epilepsy was diagnosed, but in fact Ethan's father reported that he had always been poor at sport and a messy eater. From the parents' point of view Ethan had always been a rather poorly coordinated child.

Managing emotions

Ethan's behaviour was described as attention seeking, constantly asking for reassurance and if this was not given he would sulk, refuse to do work, rip paper or barge past people. Ethan's parents confirmed that although the onset of epilepsy proved a significant barrier to Ethan's development, and the incidents of aggression increased in adolescence, in fact the antecedents of feeling socially awkward were very obvious in Ethan's day-to-day life from an early age.

Ethan was described as having an insight into his behaviour, but not as able to control his responses. He himself stated that although he liked school it was safer for him to stay in the library at break times, as this prevented him from getting into fights. He was also aware of having very few friends and said that he would like help in acquiring more. He felt friends would allow him greater opportunity for shopping trips and visits to a youth club.

Transition and transformation at Risinghill

The most immediate and identifiable transformation at Risinghill was the reduction in aggressive outbursts. Ethan stated that he wanted to be at Risinghill as it was his 'last chance' but he also felt staff did more to understand him.

Transformation through enhanced social and self-understanding

Ethan worked hard with the speech and language therapist and was prepared to work on role play to find new strategies for difficult scenarios. Staff used comic-strip conversations to help him become aware of how his sense of humour could be offensive, and although Ethan still finds this difficult to control, he is more open to reading his social stories to prepare him for social functions. Ethan can now describe the difference between personal and professional situations and he is able to modify his behaviour where a more 'professional approach' is needed.

Ethan will inevitably have difficulty in recognising the appropriateness of his actions, but he now has access to phrases which allow him to check out whether others will be offended or upset.

Ethan continues to use graphic prompts when his anxiety level is escalating. He knows when he is feeling hot and can anticipate when he will have 'fuzzy' moments. He has a number of key phrases to communicate his concerns to the group or individual such as, 'I need help now as I'm feeling unwell.'

Transformation through personalisation

Ethan liked to please staff and enjoyed adult company, but he did not like to be told what to do. Ethan finds task instruction sheets (see Chapters 5 and 7) useful because they depersonalise the situation and are non-judgemental. Ethan says he can work at his own pace and figure things out for himself and if he needs help he has learnt phrases such as 'Can I have help with this please?' or 'Could you explain that again?'

Ethan now chooses a time away card and a 'walking about' strategy that help him calm down and control his 'silly head' attitude. Ethan has identified calm colours for thinking and used art work for creating a calming picture. Ethan painted a scene where he was lying down in the grass by a winding river. He reprinted these into a postcard format and proudly gives them out to others. Ethan disliked touch and massage, although he has told his class teacher that 'Sometimes I need someone else to calm me down when my head gets out of control.'

Ethan has made good progress at home. He was provided with a support worker who helped him to travel independently on public transport and introduced him to a special needs youth club. Ethan has found a girlfriend who likes 'his smiles and his jokes', but he is aware that these might become irritating. In more reflective moments he worries that he might not be able to change as an adult, when he perceives that life will become more serious.

Transition to adulthood

Ethan gained Level 2 NVQ certificates in Business Studies and Services and is moving to a residential college.

Concluding remarks

We have tried in this chapter to give brief summary accounts of the journeys made by five of our students. These students represent the range of students that came through Risinghill – they are by no means the 'best five'. The accounts are brief and smoothed – the reality was much more variable day to day and the time frame is measured in years, rather than weeks or months. However, what we hope to have illustrated is that the future prospects for our students were transformed in that time. The adult lives that they are beginning to claim now are far different from what might have been expected at the time that they started at the school.

In the next chapter we will try to do a similar job for some of the staff members who joined us along the way. Their stories are also ones of personal growth and development and, in some cases, transformations of future prospects.

Chapter 3

THE STAFF PERSPECTIVE

This chapter will describe the experiences of some of the school staff who participated in the development of the Risinghill approach. Although we cannot mirror exactly the format used for describing the journey of the students, we will try to show how there was a similar journey for staff, how it transformed them and enabled them to transition to new career challenges. Issues of relationships, emotional management, personalisation, practicality, self-esteem and achievement we hope will come through in these accounts as it does in the students' accounts. The content is based upon personal recollections and structured interviews with the staff.

Pen pictures of five members of the leadership team at Risinghill

Susan

Susan had been a learning assistant and came to Risinghill as a 'senior support worker' with responsibility for learning assistants and residential care staff. In a previous post she had completed a diploma in autism and then during her time at Risinghill she worked towards her degree and post-graduate certificate in primary education. She was then promoted to deputy head and accepted on the National College for School Leadership course for prospective heads. Susan's style was that of a team player, who collaborated with her colleagues and helped with the completion of tasks. Susan played a key role in shaping the BERIS curricular approach (see Chapter 5). She was consistently calm with both parents and students and showed persistence in using agreed strategies with the students. Susan used modelling and shaping as a method to share her knowledge and skills with other staff. She is now head of a special school for pupils with a range of complex needs.

Diane

Diane was an experienced head of an independent mainstream secondary school in Nigeria and chose to apply for a post at Risinghill because of her interest in how the school's ethos had developed. Diane joined the leadership team as deputy head and undertook further teaching experience in order to transfer her overseas trained status into UK qualified teacher status. Diane benefited from the extensive training programme in autism at Risinghill and worked initially in collaboration with the school's experienced speech and language therapist and member of the leadership team. Diane enjoyed developing programmes for pupil motivation, applying her knowledge of psychology to the whole school approach for developing pupil self-esteem. Diane encouraged the analysis of data about pupil behaviour and excelled in refining school policies and procedures. She is now the director of the London Leadership Centre (a unit focused on approaches to school management).

Graham

Graham was an experienced teacher of students with autism, both in South Africa and then in the UK. He joined Risinghill as a deputy head with a particular responsibility for the residential curriculum and liaison with parents. Graham was particularly committed to the concept of 'real world learning' and encouraged other staff to make sure that all learning experiences were 'real' and had a firm practical base. Graham found the systems of communication at Risinghill particularly effective, especially the method of knowledge management through a comprehensive staff handbook and the importance of diary management and communication that benefited both staff and students. Graham is now the director of a special school for students with ASD and complex needs.

Elaine

Elaine came to Risinghill as an overseas trained speech and language therapist with experience of working in a school for children with severe learning difficulties and ASD. She gained certification from the UK Royal College for Speech and Language Therapists. While at Risinghill she started a teaching course to gain UK qualified teacher status. Elaine excelled at integrating her knowledge base about language and communication into the everyday functioning situations for students at Risinghill, and devising social stories to assist in student learning about difficult concepts and social relationships. Elaine completed her teacher training and became deputy head of a special school for students with ASD and complex needs.

Jane

Jane joined the staff as a learning assistant with no previous experience of autism. She had previously worked in the retail sector and so brought her experience of managing staff to developing systems and procedures at Risinghill. Jane developed a particular interest in vocational learning and the development of the NVQ (National Vocational Qualification) system for students, and then went on to train to achieve a teacher certificate in education. Jane had a collaborative style and showed great persistence in her work with difficult students. When working with students presenting challenging behaviours she took the lead on the development of mind-mapping to help students problem solve. Jane applied the psychological principles of training delivered by the school's educational psychologist, such as modelling, task analysis, reward sampling and the use of personalised rewards.

Jane became the trainer in the leadership team, helping others in learning BERIS and the Risinghill approach. She is now assistant head for pastoral care in a special school for pupils with ASD.

Reflecting on specifics
The shared approach
It was a key thrust of the senior management to develop a distinctive and shared approach to supporting the students coming to Risinghill – a house style that all staff would adopt in their work but that would be open to development in the light of growing experience. One important element was the way in which the methods described in this book evolved through practical, hands-on experimentation, together with the help of both an educational and clinical psychology perspective. This led to the development of an approach and style that could be described as a framework of support. The staff appreciated the way in which the senior management developed a shared culture, which reflected their experiences and beliefs about what works best for a range of individuals with a diagnosis of autism.

Elaine stressed the need for staff to share their knowledge and to 'keep on talking' about what works, and not to forget the importance of revisiting things that have gone well. It is so easy to fall into the trap of talking about what went wrong rather than looking for, sharing and then celebrating the ways in which the framework of support and agreed style were successful. For example the school developed a series of agreed 'mantras', which all staff were expected to use with the students together with other approaches including aromatherapy and massage, which were not necessarily part of new staff's normal practice. Staff new to a school came with a range of approaches to working with students. For some having set phrases or using calming approaches may be part of their 'natural way' of working but for many there was a need for training and support, both initial and ongoing, to implement this approach effectively. Only in this way could the necessary degree of consistency be achieved. See Appendix 1 for an example of the kind of training provided to staff.

How it feels when you first start working with students with ASD

Some staff, when they first start working with young people with autism, feel worried about working with this unknown group. The initial opportunity to see other staff modelling a clear and detailed approach right from the start was highly valued. In addition staff were given an ethos pack and a DVD with examples of the BERIS approach, to help them prepare at the start of their work in the school.

Diane was very impressed with the thought that had gone into the structure of the curriculum and the response to autism. Staff can feel that they are dropped into the deep end if they begin without knowledge and experience of autism. New senior staff described how they studied the ethos pack, assessment pack and handbook as nighttime reading, as well as reading the student files. Diane was also very reassured by the offers of help if there was anything that she did not understand. This communicated both the importance attached to the framework of support, but also the commitment to supporting staff so that they were fully able to implement it.

Jane described how she was terrified on her first day, but felt very well supported by the team – 'I started by watching all that was happening and wondering how does that all fit in. It was tiring but so much fun. Everything I put into practice now I learnt when I first started.' She recalls one experience with the system where she saw someone doing a drawing rather than speaking to a student (after she had been battling unsuccessfully with this student). The student did what he was asked and quietened down. Everything that was going on had a purpose and was supporting the pupils. The first time Jane came to the school she saw a pupil driving a tractor. She wondered why this was happening and now she can see why.

What attracted staff to work at Risinghill

Elaine was inspired by the head's passionate approach to her job, and the way in which the main interest was the students. She liked the way all staff were encouraged to think of ways to help the students make progress so that they could transition successfully into adulthood. The enthusiasm was apparent at interview and many new staff reported that this made them want to work in this school.

Another important aspect of the school's success was the regular monitoring and ongoing training, of a practical nature, within the classroom. Although for some staff the way they communicated with the children and young people in the school was natural, and appeared second nature, for most new staff it was a huge challenge. However, hearing experienced staff asking simple questions such as, 'Where is your organiser?' and then, through training, realising that such agreed mantras fitted in with the whole BERIS approach, made it possible to acquire rapidly the house style. This structure of support for staff was as important as the framework of support for students and made training an exciting and meaningful activity.

BERIS

Staff could see that the approach described as BERIS (see Chapter 5 for a fuller account of this fundamental framework) was a readily understandable way of focusing on the students, to help them live and cope with their own difficulties. It was designed with autism in mind but at the same time recognising that each young person needs an individualised approach. Staff acknowledged that many of the structures used at Risinghill, are used in other settings (things such as visual support and graphics). What made the BERIS approach unique was the way in which the things were put together. The BERIS framework helps staff in their thinking and planning, when they are putting together the individually tailored package for the student, considering his/her needs as a whole. BERIS also helps to unpick what is happening for individuals at particular times, and this natural, problem-solving method, together with referring to the agreed school style, leads to a gradual development of a tailored approach for each student. In other settings the unique needs of students with autism are not always taken into account, especially where there are no plans about how to move the students to greater independence. In contrast, at Risinghill a key aim for students was to promote their independence. For the staff, the approach clearly worked – the graphics when students were upset, the debriefing on the flip-chart, the movement activities such as massage, Sherborn and cycle track, all worked. Although at the beginning massage is a passive activity where students receive positive and nurturing touch from a member of staff, it can be shaped and developed into an activity in which there is choice by the students. Sherborn, developmental movement, is a programme that revisits early stages of motor development, allowing children to take part in floor-based games and activities such as pulling and pushing. Both these activities are aimed at helping develop a sense of self and others.

The cycle track was a circular pathway built at the end of a field, where staff would take pupils to walk as a calming down activity. Over time this became one of the key safe havens for students, who had developed an understanding that walking made a positive contribution to their ability to calm.

Another example of the way in which the students were not just passive recipients but contributed actively was when tackling a group bullying issue. This was started using a comic-strip conversations approach, but the students adapted this and put words in, or colour, so that others could understand this too.

Evolving strategies and sticking at it

One important aspect of the Risinghill approach was maintaining implementation of strategies while keeping them under discussion and review. Staff would remind each other that if a particular strategy worked with a student, not to abandon it just because an immediate situation was not resolved. Staff would report on that spirit of never under-estimating the difficulties but also never forgetting how much change can be made with the right strategies in place. Even with good strategies progress takes time.

Communication and developing insight

One intrinsic part of the Risinghill approach was to take into account the students' information processing difficulties, and to sit with students in front of a flip-chart, to discuss not just a particular event and what triggered it, but a broader perspective: how was the whole day? What has gone well? This was not an adult-led monologue, but a shared conversation and these conversations with students gave staff insight into why it is that students behave in certain ways. For instance, students saying, 'I need you to write it down,' or 'I need you to speak slowly,' or 'I need my graphics,' or 'I need a drawing to remind me.' Over time, this agreed approach became second nature to staff.

Diane was impressed by the way the system was evidently very child-centred. Prior to interview our staff training DVD made it clear that everything was being done to make the child feel comfortable; everything was thought out from the child's point of view, how to make the child's perfect day. Diane had previously worked in international education, where the students had a very strong voice and where the importance of listening was fundamental. Such an attitude is not always evident in the school experiences of pupils with ASD, as the previous chapter made clear.

Training and support

Unlike many schools, Risinghill used both the pupil-focused meetings and the regular, weekly training events to ensure that staff were given training and support about the agreed strategies and the rationale for them. For example the use of the 'How can I help?' mantra. This was intended to give the message that, 'I'm not talking at you, but you need to tell me what I can do to help make things better.' It was a way of translating the concept of joint problem solving into a practical everyday activity. Again, see Appendix 1 for an example.

Elaine commented that having applied this approach to adolescents with ASD who could express themselves verbally, this now helps her in working with younger and non-verbal students within another school. It is as much about the attitude and the stance as it is about the language used.

Monitoring and consistency

What worked at Risinghill was the consistency, and senior staff monitoring what was happening in practice. There was less a focus on what staff are supposed to do, and more on the reality of what happens and whether this works. At one level this involved sitting round, discussing, sharing different areas of knowledge about a student, identifying their specific communicative needs, their levels of anxiety, and how to find strategies that were personalised for each young person. But of course, in any setting, staff do not always follow agreed strategies (for instance, the mantras, the use of the organiser). This was overcome by senior staff observing and monitoring how all staff related to the students ('management by walking about', see Chapter 12) and ensuring that time was set aside to produce and maintain the essential equipment (such as graphics and organisers). It was also understood that as well as supporting specific practices, it was important to shape beliefs that would be compatible with these practices. Regular training and staff meetings/discussions were occasions when the principles and beliefs behind the practices were addressed. In any setting there may be some staff who have their own personal needs and issues that may get in the way of following an agreed approach. The management team were always available to talk with staff, but also gave the message that we are at work to help provide the best for the students – personal difficulties can be sympathised with and help can be offered, but they are not an excuse for poor practice. Jane explained how she learnt to keep her personal life and school life very separate.

Reconciling a set curriculum and framework of support with the need to personalise things for the individual student

The curriculum at Risinghill was unique. Its overarching purpose was to motivate the students in 'real world learning' for employability. One staff member commented on working in a previous setting (a local authority special school) which used the national curriculum and did use graphic support but where each staff member did it in his/her own way. There was no underlying philosophy and the idea was to keep the approach the same as that for other students with learning difficulties. In contrast the system at Risinghill was based upon what we know about ASD (see Chapter 4) and the experience of young people with ASD. The system was about building on the strengths of the young people and gaining insight from their personal experience. Susan talked about how, within her first week, having come from a unit for ASD attached to a mainstream school, she challenged a student who was doing something he should not have been. He picked up a huge bit of wood and swung it at her. She went back and talked to staff who knew him and this led straight into a problem-solving approach:

- Was it the environment?

- Was it something that I said?

- Had I got too close?

- How was he feeling?

- What had happened previously?

- What were the issues for the young person at the time?

It was a really fresh way of looking at things. She also appreciated the clarity of the systems in place. She knew what the expectations were in the management and education of the students. In the other school where she had worked the staff did not know what to expect of the students with ASD. In contrast at Risinghill there were very clear expectations of staff and very clear guidelines on what you were supposed to be doing. This gave a feeling of confidence in what you were doing and knowing that this was OK. There was also the very fundamental but key notion that learning could not occur unless the student was in a reasonably calm state.

Susan also learnt about staff management, how to get staff to do what you believe is right for the children. She learnt about the mutual support, trust and respect necessary for good teamwork and the importance of having a spread of skills so that team members were able to bounce ideas off each other, but also the head's commitment and drive, which energised the whole process and gave a clear sense of leadership.

While there was a general system there was also a commitment to personalisation so that the system was adapted to suit the individual person. For example if things went wrong there was a system to unpick what had happened (debriefing). The ethos was that staff should apply the system but that they also needed to be open and reflect with the student on how to improve the practice. It meant using what worked for the individual to get to the necessary information (flip-charts, comic-strip conversations, etc.) and then using what was learnt to be more proactive in the future. This in turn meant communicating the conclusions to all those involved in supporting the student. As well as these micro-developments, the system as a whole was reflected upon as a part of the regular school cycle. Thus the system could change and did evolve and this idea of continuous improvement will be revisited in Chapter 12.

From the perspective of the leadership team the systems belonged to the school not to individuals. The idea was to be sure to keep everybody in the loop involved, but also to be firm about implementation. Another fundamental shared belief was that whatever was done was about the benefit to the young people. This reality was brought to the fore when working to resolve a difference of opinion between staff. If people are there with the right intentions this also helps with everyone trusting their colleagues. The staff had a shared belief in the underlying values, but within this there was a respect for choice and individuality.

Graham talked about how staff should not be afraid to be creative, but it was vital to start with what makes sense in the real world – for example, see a real house, not a pretend house, use a real spoon not a toy spoon. He stressed the importance of generalising this to different contexts and also empowering the young people to regulate their own emotions. These were huge goals but turned out to be achievable, more so perhaps than we expected at the outset. Yet you have to keep it up and get constant feedback from the youngsters, so that it works around their needs.

Diane felt that everything she now knows about autism had been learnt at Risinghill. As a way of working, there was a lot of collaboration. Within the senior management team everything was thought out. Individuals did not do things in isolation. There was collegiality and support and there was nothing that was not shared. Everyone was given a sense of being trusted, but also being responsible. For example when it was a question of monitoring and assessing staff, senior staff did not come along with a form and 'tell' staff but worked alongside staff, planning, organising and structuring things together. Diane also valued the system for closing incidents. No matter what had happened, what the child had done, once the debrief had occurred and any consequences been decided upon then it was clearly communicated to the child that 'It is finished now,' tomorrow we start afresh. She saw this as a positive way to deal with the crises that routinely occur when supporting students such as those who came to Risinghill.

Diane also appreciated the attention to well-being of both the students and staff. She saw students as calmer and more willing to engage. Diane commented that there was not a child who came during her time there, who did not benefit from the system. It takes a bit of getting used to, it takes time, but gradually even parents reported how their children were calmer, more able to engage with people and to verbalise at home. Students might initially not even want to be touched, but end up coming to ask for massages. Again, personalisation was important so that students learnt over time what worked best for them (a massage, going to the tree house, going for a walk).

This same issue of a basic system but with personalisation was exemplified in the use of mantras, graphics and the organisers (see Chapter 7). The mantras often seemed to work better for the younger ones, for example 'It's not OK' would make some older pupils get annoyed. With the older ones more attention was needed about when, how and what to say. The organiser worked for most students. Some of the older ones felt that it marked them out as being different, but they still needed it. So it was necessary to modify it in a way that made it more discreet. Some older ones did not want to carry the graphics. Working in small groups did not suit all of them all of the time. One student opted for home education. There was nothing that did not work at all but it was an exciting and ongoing challenge to keep up the blend of system and individualisation. For staff it was both wonderful and exhausting and involved a huge amount of learning. Jane illustrates this. When she went into the older, apprentice group, Jane took away the Big Book (see Chapters 5 and 7) and started to use reminder cards, but lots of things would go wrong and things were not working out, especially at lunchtimes and arrival times. The students had learnt the routine work tasks but they could not cope in less structured times. As soon as Jane put the Big Book back up things improved in those core times, because they really needed that support. However, changes were possible. The organisers were altered, made more person-centred, giving them dividers and letting the students put them where they wanted to. They no longer needed so many graphics or mantras in their organisers. Some even abandoned them altogether in favour of notes written on sheets of paper that they carried around with them. The message was that we are in partnership with you – 'I am not going to hold your hand, but if you still have a difficulty because of your autism, I'm here to help you.' A lot of the core systems remained the same – the mantras, the Big Book, reward systems – but they were changed in line with the students' growing maturity. Jane helped to develop the use of flip-charts as an additional visual aid. She used them in a range of ways – for mind-mapping, for comic-strip conversations, making plans, to debrief after an incident, to make big graphics such as 'think' and 'stop' as well as for the more standard use for social stories. When Jane started at the school she was given a DVD and staff training book at interview, and studied it before starting. She then learnt a lot of things over time, how to deal with aggressive behaviours, to know that it is part of how the students are communicating, and about their autism. It was made clear that every single person was seen as a unique individual, that every single student was completely different, that you cannot treat them all the same way, or use the same approach for each student.

It was not all plain sailing. Some staff found the rigidity difficult, the fact that we said certain things at certain times, and the mantra process such as, 'Stop, it's not OK,' because it did not come naturally to them. We believed that using the same words gave a consistency of response. Some staff found this difficult to buy into.

Some people felt that the use of the Big Book restricted their personality. It depended upon what type of person they were as to how they responded. Jane explained that she is just the sort of person who if told to do something she will follow that method. It is part of her 'work ethic'. Other people might think what is the point of doing things, what is the benefit of it? Some staff struggled a lot with the set format (e.g. Big Book). Some people fought against being told to work in a certain way. Jane was more the sort of person who would give it a try and then say if it does not work. However, from her point of view the core, basic support systems and the BERIS approach all worked. She learnt to keep the fundamentals the same and make adaptations for different groups.

Concluding remarks

We have tried to illustrate elements of the Risinghill approach, how it evolved over time and some of the struggles. Above all we have tried to illustrate how this process influenced and was influenced by some of the individual staff. Here and in Chapter 2 we are making the point that education is not something that we do to students, but the outcome of a joint venture with our students. We are all part of a system influencing and being influenced by each other. When understood in this way the possibilities for achievement grow enormously. As Jane said: 'It has changed my life working here, it has become a vocation for me and I like working with autism.'

Chapter 4

AN UNDERSTANDING OF AUTISM

'Autistic' is a shorthand way of identifying one of the many groups of people who face tremendous difficulties in meeting the challenges of ordinary life in society as presently constructed. As a group they have attracted considerable academic and professional attention over the last 60 years or so. The group has a number of different facets that can be the focus of such attention. Autism can be viewed from a biomedical perspective, a cognitive perspective, a behavioural perspective, a sensory perspective, a motor perspective, an attachment perspective, a self-regulatory perspective...to name but a few! All of these perspectives have relevance for some purposes. There is no one right lens through which to view the phenomenon – it depends upon the questions that the viewer has in mind.

This book is about how best to educate some people identified as being on the 'autistic spectrum'. The practice described in this book is based upon a particular view of what is meant by the term autism, a view which seems most relevant to the purpose at hand (education). It is not necessarily a 'correct' or 'best' view. It is a view informed by both the research literature and by the professional experience of the authors. It is important that readers of the book understand this view as many of the practices described derive from it. There can be other views and other practices. There is no one right view, one right way. This is just how the authors see it and how the specific practices described were developed.

The concept of autism...in its place

An individual acquires the label 'autistic' when other people observe a number of characteristics of that individual's behaviour when young, in the first five years or so of life. Sometimes the word is acquired later in life, but even then early history is critical to the judgement being made. There are no biological tests involved – no blood tests, no brain scans, no EEGs. There are only behavioural observations. Experts have agreed the list of characteristics that need to be considered – and the individual has to have a certain number of these characteristics for the label to be applied according to the rules laid down by professional groups who consider themselves as experts. The main characteristics are:

- Difficulty in forming reciprocal social relationships, sometimes accompanied by an apparent lack of interest in these relationships.

- Difficulty with verbal and non-verbal communication, both expressive and receptive.

- Play that lacks imaginative elements.

- A strong attachment to routines, rituals and structure and a strong dislike of change.

- A key focus of interest to the exclusion of all other interests (obsessions).

- Unusual and repetitive motor movements.

You can have some of these characteristics, but if you do not have enough as decided by the experts the word 'autism' cannot rightly be applied. Autism is defined by these characteristics – there is not something else beyond the characteristics. Autism does not underlie these characteristics – it is these characteristics. It is not a disease or an illness, it is a behavioural category into which people can be sorted (or not) according to the determination rules laid down. There are of course millions of such categories into which people can be sorted – height, eye colour, handedness, academic ability, practical ability, personality types, gender, ethnicity, culture…the list is endless. To describe any individual adequately would require locating them in a vast multidimensional space of individual categories. Autism is a small star in a huge galaxy.

However, this small star can seem like the only sun. 'Diagnosis' remains a very important enterprise but the label can come to overshadow the individual. He comes to be defined entirely as 'autistic' – everything he does or is like comes to be attributed to 'autism'. One's whole life can be so determined as you find yourself spending all your school years and adult years in the company of other people in the same category, whether or not you as a person have much in common with other group members, other than your group membership. Left handers (or should we say 'people who suffer from sinistralism') beware! Allocating someone to the category 'autistic' presents therefore a significant challenge for others to be able to see the millions of other categories that can be applied to this person and that together will enable a full understanding of this person. You cannot know the individual just by knowing the diagnosis. You cannot support an individual just on the basis of the diagnosis. Differences between individuals are as important as the things that they have in common. It is an irony that autism can trigger an obsessional focus in others that gets in the way of effective supports for the individual concerned.

This catergorising should aim to get beyond the behavioural descriptors that determine 'diagnosis' and to try to understand the underlying processes, what is actually going on for the person. If some understanding of what drives the behaviour can be achieved then we are in a better position to provide relevant help and support.

Thus in our work to help people with this label on their journey in life it is vital to understand what underlies or drives this way of being. However, it is equally important to understand that we are working for a real human being not a diagnosis and that our starting point for effective support must be getting to know the person first, the diagnosis second.

People first

At the heart of any person-to-person work is the ability to understand who the person is based upon information we have about her, and to find some empathic connection with that person. Working for people identified as autistic, we are often unable to gather this information and build this connection in the usual way – by conversations with the individual. We can do this with some people who have well-developed verbal skills but even in these cases, as in all others, we also need access to information from others who know the person well. These will often be parents in the first instance but will include any who have spent/currently spend a lot of time with the person in question (see Smull and Allen 1999). Once we have the information then we have to reflect upon that information and use imagination to access some sense of who the person is and how it is for her. To person-centre our view, some of the key areas of information needed are:

- *Personality* – outgoing/shy, anxious/mellow, volatile/laidback, amenable/not amenable, caring/self-focused.

- *Preference spread* – things that are important to the person, things he actively seeks/avoids, things he seems to like/dislike, topics he most commonly communicates about (however, he is able to communicate).

- *Thinking style* – focused/unfocused, serial tasker/multitasker, slow pace/fast pace, perfectionist, positive emphasiser/negative emphasiser (Tigger and Eeyore!).

- *Ability spread* – strengths and weaknesses in a range of abilities.

- *Culture and ethnicity* – general descriptors and the specific activities that are important to that cultural group.

- *Personal history* – significant life events that include major changes/ transitions, triumphs, losses and traumas.

- *Good day/bad day* – what factors contribute to having a good or bad day, which specific days tend to be good or bad, how would one create a 'perfect' day.

- *Support network* – the range of people in the social network, their closeness, role and attitudes towards the person and an overall sense of how securely the person is 'held' by this network.

Without access to this kind of information it will be impossible to have any sense of the individual. But the information itself is only one part of the process. The objective information gathered needs to be reflected upon and time given to seeking a more empathic sense of the other (Clements and Martin 2002). Such information and the struggle for empathy that goes with it will impact significantly the quality of the relationship formed. Without this work the relationship may come to be based just upon the 'autism' and a stereotyped view of what people with this label need. This in turn impacts the competence of the support offered. We are more likely to achieve the goals we set out to achieve if we have access to this information and give time to forming an empathic connection than if we do not engage in this way.

So a focus on getting to know and understand the person as an individual is always the starting point for any competent helping relationship. However, it is undoubtedly the case that people categorised as autistic face huge challenges in making their way through life in a way that brings them satisfaction and a sense of self-worth. It is a hard road to walk. The ordinary things in life, that others take so much for granted, require hard work and immense courage from the people that we are categorising in this way. We therefore do need to understand the challenges that people face, the ways that autism affects the journey through life, if we are to have a comprehensive understanding of the individual and how to be helpful to them. We also need to be aware that 'autism' can mean gifts as well as burdens and be alert to the strengths that people bring to the challenges that they face.

Back to autism – the drivers of what we observe

The work described in this book is based upon an understanding that certain key processes underlie many, although not all, of the things that we observe and regard as different about people with autism. We do not propose a theory of autism, but a few understandings that can be helpful in devising practical supports in the context of education for young people growing up. These processes are as follows.

Disrupted attachment mechanisms

We see the social difficulties associated with autism as deriving from the normal attachment mechanism being damaged. Without this mechanism the infant struggles to connect with his parents in the way that has evolved as preferable over human history. From this initial difficulty in forging the earliest attachments, certain predictable outcomes result (see Rutter, Kreppner and Sonuga-Barke 2009 for a review of this area).

- A generalised difficulty with and variable motivation to engage with others.

- The failure to develop easily the core understandings about how other people think and feel and incorporate that knowledge in to how we relate (problems with the so-called theory of mind).

- A high need for control – cut off from such a central early relationship the child becomes focused on solving all problems alone, does not learn that other people can help (indeed they seem rather intrusive and bothersome), finds the world overwhelming and tries to manage all that by controlling the world…or rather creating a controllable world.

- A major problem with understanding and regulating emotions – a key task in early attachments is the management of distress and discomfort. Self-regulation develops because initially someone else responded to the distress, made sense of it and relieved it. The emotional world was made understandable and manageable. Cut off from that experience, the child with autism finds distress incomprehensible and unmanageable. Thus distress quickly escalates out of control and such loss of control is implicated in some of the extreme behaviours that some people with autism display.

It is not that people on the autistic spectrum do not form relationships and attachments. They clearly do. It is just that the normal ways of doing this are disrupted and that leads to the sorts of outcomes described above.

Selective information processing difficulties

People on the autistic spectrum can experience a number of difficulties in processing information (there is a huge literature about this, e.g. Volkmar *et al.* 2005).

- Many, but not all, find difficulty in processing verbally encoded information, in terms of both messages coming in and of communicating out to others. Visual processing can be much stronger. However, given our cultural preference for verbal communications these problems present a major challenge for people with autism and lead to a lot of communication breakdowns.

- There are often problems in depth of processing, extracting deeper or more abstract meanings from what is presented. This again leads to communication breakdowns as the person will fail to spot 'hidden' meanings and thus misunderstand what others are trying to convey. The flip-side of this problem is that processing is strong for literal interpretation and clear, direct forms of communication.

- This problem with extracting information at multiple levels also shows up in a difficulty with problem solving and thinking round novel situations – a difficulty in identifying possibilities and alternatives and integrating information from different areas. On the other hand we must not forget that there are tremendous strengths in rote learning and rule learning and an infinite capacity to take on board specific and concrete items of information.

Emotional imbalance – the challenge to maintain a sense of positive well-being

Emotional difficulties are very central to our understanding of people with autism (Clements 2005). Some of these difficulties are direct, some indirect.

- One of the direct difficulties is the emotional dysregulation described above that means distress once evoked often gets out of control. Added to this is the fact that there are many more sources of distress for a person with autism compared to others, so that the experience of loss of control is more frequent, leading in turn to some feeling chronically stressed.

- Distress may derive from the difficulties in understanding situations and social requirements, the difficulties in understanding that life requires accommodation to others not just the pursuit of one's own goals, the difficulties in understanding oneself, one's needs and both how to communicate these needs but more deeply not understanding that others can be of help with those needs. These kinds of incomprehension are fertile ground for aversive experiences.

- There are, for many, sensory issues (see below) which again make situations that are ordinary for others aversive for the person identified as autistic.

- Basic research seems to indicate some kind of genetic link between autism and depression and we certainly know that people identified as autistic are vulnerable to bouts of depression.

In addition to the direct, primary difficulties mentioned above, there are a range of indirect difficulties caused by other factors.

- As already mentioned ordinary life contains more triggers for distress among people with autism compared to others.

- As a group they are more vulnerable to abusive experiences of all kinds (physical, emotional, sexual) and, in particular, are very vulnerable to bullying and teasing in school to the point of traumatic damage.

These difficulties mean that it is very challenging for a person identified as on the autistic spectrum to maintain a sense of positive well-being. Without this sense of well-being it is very hard to meet the challenges of everyday life – to be motivated to persevere, to do the hard work, to show the courage required. Lack of well-being will mean increased irritability, increased resistance to trying new things, more rumination on negative things and increased compulsive tendencies. Lack of well-being contributes very directly to the more serious behavioural challenges (aggression, self-injury, property damage) that are associated with autism. Finally it is important to note that having high abilities and good verbal skills does not provide improved resilience in the autism context. People with Asperger's syndrome/high functioning autism are as or more likely to experience emotional and behavioural difficulties as those who may be regarded as much more significantly disabled.

These are the main perspectives that inform the work described in this book. There are other difficulties that affect people with autism. Sensory processing difficulties are much written about. While our understanding of these issues has informed our practice at the common sense level it has not been central to evolving the support mechanisms described in this book. Movement control difficulties are obvious in quite a number of people with autism, some of whom can also be diagnosed with Tourette's syndrome. It is an important area and relevant to some forms of challenging behaviour, especially self-injury. However, our understanding of the mechanisms is limited and the practical implications for supporting people on a day-to-day basis have yet to be fully explored. Certainly the practices described in this book reflect a limited understanding of this area and some movement-related work is described, but it has not been as central to our practice as the other areas that we have been discussing. Finally biomedical difficulties are an area of intense interest at the present time, but have not been influential on the work that we have undertaken.

From understanding to practice – a preview

Given our understanding of what is going on for people with autism, our 'autism' practice emphasises three key areas:

1. *Strong and positive relationships* – we see the relationship difficulties not as indicating the need to leave people alone, but as indicating the need to redouble our efforts to form strong bonds and attachments. From our own experience and our reading of the literatures on autism, parenting styles, schizophrenia and attachment disorder, we see certain characteristics of relationship style that are important when normal attachment mechanisms are damaged (see for example, Hughes 2006). These characteristics include a degree of intrusiveness and perseverance, an often expressed wish to help rather than control, empathy especially an understanding of how hard this is for the person with autism, an element of playfulness and fun, clarity in communication, firmness in certain boundaries and low expressed emotion. There is a need to avoid high authoritarianism and punitiveness, but on the other hand the other extreme of accommodation without limits is also to be avoided. Warm and authoritative are perhaps the words that best apply.

2. *Effective information transmission* – at the verbal level this involves limited use of language, an emphasis on literal information and clear rules, but a challenge to think and to find ways of representing

concretely more abstract or 'invisible' information. Behind the verbal communication there has to be a comprehensive commitment to back up and present as much information as possible in a visual format. This may not be the natural way, particularly for educators who often find verbal communications their automatic style. Nevertheless staff and parents need to work at finding visual communications wherever possible.

3. *The promotion of positive well-being* – this involves inducting positive states for the individual on a regular basis, finding meaningful learning that makes the student feel valued, communicating directly and through rewards how much we value the student and the work that she does, building an understanding of what emotions are and how they are caused, using post-incident debriefing to develop an understanding of what went on and what lessons can be learnt. These are all practice elements that follow from our understanding of how difficult it is for the person identified as autistic to maintain a positive sense of well-being…and how central this is to her success in life.

This is just a brief preview of the practices that will be described in Chapters 5 to 10. It illustrates the link between the practices and how we view that category of experience that is called 'autism'.

Chapter 5

ETHOS, PRACTICE AND CURRICULUM

The approach described in this book combines a general school ethos with a specific curriculum that prioritised both content and the way in which learning outcomes were to be achieved. The elements evolved over many years and what is presented here is a 'progress report' – the story so far. The evolution was powered by experience and the strong belief of the headteacher that applied psychology (educational and clinical) had a central role in educational practice. More specifically, some of the early influences on the work with students (from the 1980s on) included the Portage approach, positive approaches to work with parents (Westmacott and Cameron 1981) and the EDY (Education of the Developmentally Young) programme developed at the Hester Adrian Research Centre. Portage is a model of regular home-visiting, which involves working with parents to set clear and relevant outcomes, planning daily activities following a task analysis and the use of long-term goals (Dessent 1984; Frohman, Weber and Wollenburg 1983). EDY explores the ways in which staff can change through micro-analysis of their teaching approaches, including learning to prepare and present activities in appropriate ways and devising methods of prompt and praise that suit the individual child (McBrien, Farrell and Foxen 1992). There were similar influences on the support for staff from an extensive literature in the 1970s and 1980s (Clements 1987). We are delighted to acknowledge and to celebrate these historical influences that are all too easy to forget in 'modern times'.

The general ethos
The headteacher of the school had a belief that her school could meet the diverse needs of the children and young people with ASD, but that for this to occur it was necessary to empower the whole staff group with a continuous programme of training and development. There was a belief that all staff members are equally important, and that teachers and support staff share the responsibility as educators and should have equal access to training. Finally, long before 'personalisation' became a buzzword in the UK, the head believed that her staff group could achieve success for all the

students with ASD only if there were regular opportunities throughout the week to reflect on the individual needs of each pupil and to plan for their learning and development. In the planning it would be critical always to consider the impact of the environment and how that interacted with the individual pupil.

Specific practices

This ethos both drove and was refined by a number of more specific inputs. The educational psychologist delivered hands-on practical training in how to teach students with ASD on a one-to-one basis. This included how to undertake a functional analysis, different ways of planning the analysis of a task, reward assessment, planning and presentation of tasks, as well as taking care that staff agreed and then set realistic targets within a time frame. Staff were filmed working with students and this was then analysed by the staff and the educational psychologist together to highlight whatever aspect of learning theory was being worked on and how that approach had worked for the individual student. Once success was achieved in individual sessions staff then had to plan for generalisation to other settings.

As well as focusing on staff, the work of the school also recognised the need to build in work with parents. Early on the head and some staff were trained in Portage methods, so that activity charts were written first for all staff to use when teaching a particular skill, and then discussed and agreed with parents to plan for generalisation at home.

Work with both educational and clinical psychologists influenced the way in which staff agreed the need for clear and consistent boundary setting and communication with the students to make it obvious that it was the adults that set the rules. This in turn led to the development of a range of communication aids carried by both staff and students – staff carried laminated messages and schedules in a bum bag, and students carried a personal organiser and a back pack. As a part of the Risinghill style of communication, if a pupil appeared to be finding something difficult, staff would use a flip-chart to explore collaboratively with the student what had happened and how the problem might be solved. Social stories were used to help students reflect on what had happened and this later developed into the use of mind-mapping as a planning tool for students when discussing how they saw issues and how they might tackle new learning opportunities.

The initial aims for the specialist curriculum were to ensure that children were:

- in control of their feelings
- in charge of their learning
- responsible for their actions.

Theory of Mind research helped us to understand that when working with students with ASD we needed to transform the private act of thinking into a public display. We understood that in our teaching we needed to 'role play' and constantly model how to:

- think and talk about your thoughts and feelings
- think and plan about relating to others
- develop strategies for attending and calming
- think about tasks
- organise information
- sequence tasks
- decide what to do next.

As the Risinghill approach evolved, the head and senior staff, together with their educational psychologist, agreed upon an acronym to help new staff at the point of induction grasp what the school was about. This mnemonic was BERIS. BERIS refers to the following five areas:

- Body Basics.
- Environment.
- Relatedness.
- Insight.
- Self-belief.

BERIS explained
Body Basics
This part of the curriculum helped students to reflect upon 'What does your body feel like?', 'What does it feel like to be calm and relaxed?', 'How do you position your body to promote attending to an activity?' This curriculum also helped the staff to reflect upon how they could best position themselves and lay out activities to be most helpful for the students (for example taking into account if a student is left-handed). One very important part of the Body Basics curriculum was planning for movement

through unstructured times, for example developing spatial awareness when some students are walking near the cycle track while others are cycling along it. Staff were encouraged to set the expectation that pupils walked briskly from one location in the school to another.

At Risinghill, touch as a teaching tool was viewed as a positive strategy, which included the use of physical and gestural prompting. In more structured settings such as the kitchen, staff would seek the student's permission before prompting, such as when using hand over hand prompting when, for example, learning how to whisk. An extension of this approach was the use of massage for calming, communication and achieving relaxation. A 'Touchtalks' programme was developed using massage stories and this will be described in Chapter 9.

Environment

Many students with ASD have a fundamental difficulty coping with different environments. They vary considerably in what motivates them and what activities they choose to participate in. For example one student chose to collect golf balls as a reward for completing a sorting task within the business administration work environment. Students with ASD are well known for their difficulties in self-organisation. Risinghill built upon the TEACCH principles and developed a range of topics aiming for 'real world learning'. This in practice meant building the curriculum upon current events. For instance, students were given jobs with the aim that they complete them as independently as possible. A job such as preparing vegetables could be broken down into a range of tasks, such as washing, peeling and chopping. Task instruction sheets were written that could be followed by a range of students (see the example below for tying an apron, Figure 5.1). For more complex tasks individual activity charts were produced, planned after having observed the baseline functioning level of the child. Sometimes specialised techniques such as backward chaining were used. What was really important at Risinghill was to plan for generalisation so that students were able to practise tasks (such as putting on and doing up their shoes independently) throughout the school day. This was helped by having a range of different uniforms to designate particular roles and tasks at school, such as catering, horticulture and business administration.

Task Instructions

My Name: Dean   Date: 01/10/06

My task is...	To put on an apron for catering	
I am doing this because	wearing an apron keeps my clothes clean and is a Health & Safety rule	
To finish the task I will have to...	1	put the loop over my head
	2	wrap the 2 straps behind
	3	swap the straps from one hand to the other behind me
	4	Bring the straps round to the front
	5	Tie the straps in a knot and pull it tight
	6	Tie a second knot
I will need...	A clean apron A mirror	
I have finished when...	My apron is securely tied My supervisor has checked	

Task completed satisfactorily

When I've finished my task I must:

- See my supervisor to get the task signed off
- Put this instruction sheet in my 'Finished Work' tray
- Check my organiser to see what happens next.

Figure 5.1 Example of task instruction sheet

The students were helped to understand that there would be tasks set throughout the day's programme that required different approaches. Staff used a Big Book which laid out what was planned for each session and this then helped the students understand what was expected, such as:

- The start of the session explaining the session format.
- The purpose of the session.
- What would happen during the session.
- What equipment was needed.

The Big Book also made it clear at the start of the session who was the Big Talker (who would lead the session), who was the shaper (there to help individual students), what was expected to be achieved in the lesson and how they would know it was finished (see Figures 5.2 and 5.3).

Figure 5.2 The Big Book: Example 1

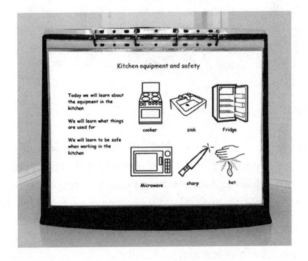

Figure 5.3 The Big Book: Example 2

Other aspects of the basic communication kit included:

- The planner/organiser.
- Key ring graphics.
- Thinking cards.
- The flip-chart or white board to support the development of long-term memory by creating visual patterns of what was discussed.

The planner

The planner/organiser is essentially an information processing system. It is a 'book of knowledge' of the strategies that will help each individual. It became a profile of themselves. Making children familiar with their thinking and ideas invites children to find solutions for difficulties. The planner needs to be a constant source of reference. Children need to be shown how to use the planner. Teaching should allow children to start to think about how they can convert information into a format that makes sense to them.

In using the planner, our task was to help disorganised or rigid thinkers understand how to:

- search and store information systematically
- select the relevant information
- remember
- imagine – what to do next.

Such a planner can take a number of forms, but it needs to be portable so that children can continue to learn in all the various school environments and away from school. It is essential that as many adults as possible, including parents and carers, are convinced of the value of using a toolkit of ideas that will support the children to become independent thinkers.

Some habits and rituals that children develop are stress reducing and useful; however, others can be limiting. The format of the planner supports children to move from being rigid and disorganised into learning about information gathering.

Key ring graphics

Our lives are full of visual supports. Adults need to respect and acknowledge the importance of the visual in helping us make sense of what to do, for example, queue here, wash your hands now. We need to point these out in order to help children realise that graphics are for everyone. Small graphics are easily carried on a key ring by staff to remind children that they can ask for help or request anything that will help their thinking and adults will respond.

Thinking cards

Thinking cards are used as a self-prompt for the student. For example Dean now uses a thinking card to help him when asked a question by an adult – it reminds him to count to ten and then ask certain things, such as, 'Can you say that again please?', 'Can you write it down?', 'Sorry, I don't understand.' Other students might be reminded to break jobs down into small timed tasks or be reminded about how to stand and look when talking to an adult.

The flip-chart/white marker board

Writing or drawing creates a way of thinking about different perspectives and alternatives. This is an extension for thinking, a way of externalising the process and showing that you value different ideas. The adult can present the concepts of:

- Who thinks/feels what…and why?
- What can we do – what else can we try?
- What is the alternative?
- What choices do we have?
- What are the plus/minus/interesting facts?
- What are the easy/hard/never tried before ideas?

Relatedness

In the area of relatedness the students were learning that their actions connect with others, that there are rules about what they can do with others and that there are ways in which they can ask for help if needed. The role of the adult is seen as modelling and making visible this whole process of thinking and helping to reduce a student's level of anxiety by creating graphic or social stories. Staff used a range of methods to help with relatedness. They drew line drawings of named students with thought bubbles representing different perspectives. If the student came up with a novel idea, the staff would say, 'I didn't know that was what you were thinking.' For instance, Colin would feel anxious when food was being passed around a group because he was concerned there would be none left for him. His thoughts and feelings could be drawn out and then linked to something he could do to relieve his anxiety (for example, remind people to leave some for him). Staff would help students plan how to ask relevant questions by drawing speech bubbles. If the student needed to have a prompt to write it down, a pencil shape would remind him to write something that that felt too emotional to say. Also, when there was a change to the planned programme everyone would use a green sticker or green pen to highlight the change on the organiser. This helped the students see that the adult is a helper in the environment and they can then facilitate any problem solving that might be needed.

To create a style of working where connections are public and obvious meant creating a style of working where the adult and child share a focus. The connection between various forms of communication – thinking, talking and writing – was illustrated constantly, as was the role of the adult as helper. So, for example if things go wrong, the sympathetic adult uses the communication tools to help explain differences in thinking and explain where things went wrong. This procedure tackles failure as a stage in thinking – acknowledging that something went wrong. It allows honesty. Examples of phrases an adult can use are:

- I didn't know that.

- Can you help me understand?

- I'm thinking this because…

Insight

With insight we wanted to help the students to develop insights about their strengths and to reflect on the success of their interactions. For example, students looked at videos of particular, real life scenarios, and then worked with an adult to reflect upon what they were thinking, and what they needed to tell the staff that would help them to work with the student. For example Alan could not understand that when a certain member of staff was not giving him attention, the staff member was not being hostile and ignoring him but rather was preparing for a session. Colin needed help to understand that when he walked into somebody's room, without a verbal or gestural communication, he needed to indicate in some way the reason for him being there. He was taught a way of knocking on a door and saying hello.

Mind-mapping, a way of recording key thoughts and exploring shared thinking patterns (see Figures 7.4 and 7.5), was a development from scripted social stories to joint problem solving with adults. It builds on the idea that everyone has a different viewpoint and that these can be combined into an agreed plan for the future. Mind-mapping was used for a range of purposes, such as planning an outing with a group to a shop to carry out a functional task, while addressing individual student's concerns. It was also used to help students reflect on their emotions and on events that happened.

Self-belief

The staff encouraged students to come to them to celebrate a success. This became a part of the school culture in which staff gave genuine, enthusiastic praise. All the time staff would make positive comments about what they saw the students achieving, and this linked to the long-term aims that had been agreed at reviews; reviews which actively involved the students.

Since celebration was part of the Risinghill culture, staff would always find out from the students what their preferred reward would be. As well as specific and immediate rewards, throughout the different age groups there was a regular weekly ceremony where students were given certificates for their achievements. At sharing events with parents there were celebrations for achievement and participation in activities. Over the years at Risinghill the students would go on a journey from needing tangible and immediate rewards to being able to defer the need for a reward until they got a special treat at a later date. Some students would like their parents to be part of a points-based reward system that they were using at school.

To illustrate concretely the impact of this culture of celebration, all the students described in Chapter 2 moved from showing a bland, low affect facial expression to big, beaming smiles when they had achieved something. Colin began to say, 'I'm proud' when he was talking about his improved behaviour, the fact that he could now keep his 'sensible head' on most of the time and was more in control of his behaviour. For Alan and Ben their increased self-belief was evident as they matured. Alan returned to the school after attending horticultural college with great pride in all that he had achieved. He is now going back to college to get more qualifications. He is transformed in his self-belief: he now knows that he can manage both his own learning and his behaviour. For Ben he has been transformed from an under-confident, overweight and anxious teenager, to a happy, slim and fit young man who has been successful in staying in a four-year apprenticeship scheme in motor-mechanics.

The BERIS approach focuses on the process of learning rather than on just the content of a particular imposed curriculum. It aims to make the children and young people active participants in their own learning, confident in their ability to handle situations and to develop an overall view of themselves as successful people. Both their achievements and the way they talk about themselves testifies to the transformation that has occurred.

Chapter 6

THE RELATIONSHIP STYLE

Teaching is about being effective in the relationship between teacher and student – it is about engaging and motivating the student, making information accessible but also challenging and stretching the student. It is about setting limits and maintaining order. Although relationships are influenced by all the parties involved, in teaching (as in parenting) the onus is more on one party (the teacher) to make that relationship work.

Effectiveness in relationships can be studied at a number of levels. It can be broken down into highly specific skills:

- How we stand.
- Where our hands are.
- Eye contact.
- When and how we speak.
- The language we use.
- Tone of voice.
- Giving feedback.
- Levying consequences.

There are plenty of books about friendship, good manners, parenting, teaching, coaching and leadership that focus on specific aspects of behaviour, advising on the do's and don'ts of being effective in particular social situations.

However, it is also possible to consider relating at a broader level, in terms of what we might call relationship style. A relationship style is a whole pattern of behaviours, verbal and non-verbal, sometimes including thought processes and internal feelings, that an individual exhibits with some consistency either across situations (the person always relates in the same sort of way no matter what the situation) or over time in the same situation (I might have a certain style as a psychologist which is shown when I am being a psychologist which is different to my style when I am being a parent or when I am being a fan, watching a rugby game!). A lot of interest in relationship style is focused upon styles that enable one to be especially effective in particular roles such as being a parent. Research would tend to suggest that parents who fulfil the following criteria have children who are more advanced and better adjusted. They:

- are available to their children
- watch them a lot
- play with and talk to them
- stimulate them and explain things to them
- discuss 'hidden' matters like thoughts and feelings
- remain on a relatively even emotional keel but set clear, firm and consistent limits.

More recently this kind of research has looked at infants and younger children and found similar behaviour, attitude and emotional factors that are more likely to promote strong attachments between child and parent (e.g. Sears and Sears 2009). In the completely different field of counselling, research has looked at the verbal and non-verbal behaviours and mind sets that are associated with clients gaining benefit from the counselling relationship (see Truax and Carkhuff 1967 for a seminal text). Here the key features are described as:

- non-directive
- showing empathy, warmth and genuineness.

In the world of business there has been a similar interest in leadership styles that are best suited to corporate success. It is beyond the scope of this book to examine in detail the validity of the claims that certain styles produce better outcomes in any given situation. The point made is that there appear to be definable style categories and that many think that some styles are more 'fit for purpose' than others, in terms of achieving positive outcomes in specific roles (being a parent of a young child, being a counsellor, being a corporate leader).

This approach can be refined to consider whether there are styles that are best suited to particular types of individuals with whom one is trying to engage in a constructive relationship. Here the question is not so much the style that achieves the best outcomes as a parent, counsellor or corporate leader, but rather whether a style is best suited to being a parent of a particular type of child; a counsellor to a particular type of client; a leader in a particular type of organisation. Thus in the mental health field there has been considerable research showing that people who have had a breakdown of the schizophrenic type are more likely to relapse if looked after in family situations marked by high 'expressed emotion' – where people express their feelings openly and intensely as and when they feel them, where conflict, criticism and hostility are overt (see Leff and Vaughn 1985 for an early summary of what is now a very big field of research). Where people act in a more emotionally controlled or repressed way this seems to help the affected individual to maintain positive functioning. Closer to the situations described in this book there has been interest in how best to parent children with an attachment disorder as ordinary parenting can be ineffective with these children. Dan Hughes has been an influential voice in this respect (Hughes 2006). Among the many things thought to be constructive in parenting such children are:

- The need for empathy with the child.

- Tight control of the emotions the child can provoke.

- Very clear rules and limits with consequences attached.

- Consequences delivered in a matter of fact way.

- An emphasis to the child that what he does reflects the choices that he makes (rather than reflecting his terrible background or his disturbed brain).

- Looking for the chance to have enjoyment and fun and be playful.

- Careful use of paradox (challenging the child to do what in fact you do not want him to do).

That is just a brief summary of a complex area, but it illustrates how a style can be fitted to the particular needs of an individual rather than there being a one size fits all notion of 'parenting'.

Relationship style at Risinghill

It would be misleading to suggest that the work at Risinghill began with a clear notion of a relationship style best suited to the needs of the young people with autism attending the school. Rather, as the work developed and progressed it became clear that we were in fact adopting a particular style towards the children and were expecting new staff to take on this style, not just the specific interventions for each child. The style that emerged had several specific components and as we identify those the reader will see a lot of overlap with the work of Hughes, although at the time we were not aware of this work. The style included a range of attitudes and a number of specific behaviours. Some of the most important elements are described below.

Attitudes

I'm here to help: The staff were encouraged to see themselves as helpers rather than controllers. Help was conceived as an active and directive process rather than a passive process and was offered within a structured framework of tasks, rules and consequences (see below). It was a matter of joint problem solving rather than didactic inputs from an expert. This attitude would be expressed in a range of verbal and non-verbal behaviours, most noticeable when managing conflict situations with the student.

I know things are hard for you: The need for empathy was stressed based upon a clear understanding of autism as well as the specific circumstances of the individual student.

I will do my best to make things comfortable for you: Following from empathy is the emphasis on trying to help students be comfortable. However, this is combined with the following attitudes too.

There are choices and consequences: The behaviours you engage in reflect the choices that you make and there are consequences attached to these choices. I will do my best to help you make smart choices, but in the end it will be your choice. Autism may be an explanation of many things but it is an excuse for nothing.

I will repair breakdowns: There will be conflict and things will go wrong and it will be my job to organise us to reflect on those incidents, learn from them and move on.

Behaviours

Emotional control: Staff were expected to maintain a matter of fact approach and control their own feelings, but also reflect back the feelings they saw the students experiencing.

Challenging the students to think: Rather than directing students all the time, staff were expected to challenge them to think and to make choices.

Repetition: A lot of repetition was expected in terms of 'core messages' which were encoded into mantras for the staff to use in situations as they arose (for example, 'it's not OK').

Delivering consequences: Staff were expected to deliver consequences in accordance with the rules of the system.

Visual communication: As part of the commitment to helping, staff used a very wide range of visual communication strategies – they were expected to learn these and to use them routinely.

Well-being practice: The empathy attitude linked to a wide range of practices designed to enhance well-being and maintain comfort, and staff were expected to learn and to implement these practices.

Incident debriefing: After a confrontation had been managed it was expected that there would be a debriefing with the student to see what could be learnt, how the incident came about and what we could do to avoid it happening again.

In the subsequent chapters these specific practices will be examined in more detail. However it is important for the reader to understand that those practices were embedded in and grew out of an overall culture and set of attitudes that pervaded the organisation. Staff were not just expected to implement the practices but implement them in the style outlined above.

It might be thought that the above description of relationship style is no more than common sense and general good practice. Would that it were so! Even a modicum of experience will indicate that students with autism can be subject to a wide range of styles. Common alternatives that are used but, in our view, are not helpful to young people with autism include the authoritarian style, the laissez-faire style and the nurturing care style.

Authoritarian style

Underlying this model are the notions that autism makes it impossible for you to think properly and may easily lead you to get out of control. Staff are therefore to focus on being in control, being highly directive and structuring time but with no explanations. Choices are limited to the trivial (squash or water?). Behaviour is linked to consequences but without explanation or reflection. Staff are free to raise their voices and generally express their own feelings, particularly negative ones. Confrontational body language is also supported in this style.

Laissez-faire style

Based on no understanding of autism and the glibbest understanding of any human behaviour, this relegates staff to the passive role of deciding/ teaching nothing, setting no limits and supporting whatever choices the individual makes...until those choices result in such inappropriate actions that the person with autism is normally ejected from the system. Staff have a general attitude of respect for the other, control their own emotions and adopt non-confrontational body language. They are essentially passive.

Nurturing care style

This is based on an understanding of autism as a crippling pathology, as a matter of overwhelming sadness. The emphasis is on comfort not challenge, and nurturing may be encouraged, even to the point of intrusiveness. Expectations for change and development are low or absent, difficult challenges are avoided and there is no emphasis on rules, limits and consequences. There will certainly be emotional engagement and an emphasis on empathy. Staff will be expected to control their own negative feelings and not engage in confrontational approaches. Comfort without challenge is perhaps the best way of summarising this style.

Concluding remarks

Although relationship styles are readily observable, they are hardly discussed at all in the specialist literature on autism. Part of the function of this chapter is to emphasise the topic as one worthy of discussion. It has very important implications for how we train and support staff and could in turn increase the access of people with autism to effective help. At present effective help is described either in terms of specific techniques or in terms of the magic of charismatic individuals. Relationship style is a concept that can help to bridge that gap by showing how specific techniques become maximally effective when they are incorporated into an overall relationship that fits with those techniques. That is the hope anyway. It will be for future research to establish the merits of relationship style as a concept and/or whether specific styles are particularly effective for people with autism (or not). At this stage we do not know for sure, but it seems a plausible avenue to explore and emerged strongly from our experience of working with the young people who are the focus of this book.

Chapter 7

RELATIONSHIP TECHNIQUES – VISUAL SUPPORTS FOR COMMUNICATION

One of the main aims of our approach at Risinghill was to communicate effectively, immediately and unambiguously with the students. The visual support systems described in this chapter were our specific tools for achieving this aim. They are either prepared in advance of the lesson, or during the lesson together with the students, or, because they reflect the school ethos, are part of the staff's toolkit and are unchanging.

The initial aims in designing the curriculum at Risinghill were to ensure that children were:

- in control of their feelings
- in charge of their learning
- responsible for their actions.

Our knowledge of the way the minds of young people with ASD work and their tendency to get easily distracted and diverted by other things and their own agenda, helped us to understand that when working with these students we needed to transform the private act of thinking into a public display. We realised that as teachers we needed to 'role play' and constantly model how to:

- think about tasks
- organise information
- sequence tasks
- decide what to do next.

All the visual supports described below are designed to help us work with students so as to keep their focus on thinking about and attending to the task in hand. The use of visual supports is there to build shared tools for communication between students and staff. The systems ensure that there is no need for guesswork, that staff and other students do not need to 'mind read' in order to find out what an individual thinks and wants.

The Big Book

The Big Book (see Figure 7.1) is a pre-prepared tool that links thinking skills into effective problem solving in real life situations. It takes the key elements of a teaching session, including what the purpose is and what is going to happen. These include:

- The overall aim and purposes of the session.

- Information on how the session will be structured.

- The relevance of session tasks and, at the end of the session, a review of what has been learnt.

The Big Book sets out simply what the tasks are, with a picture and corresponding object (for lower functioning children) and what staff are there to help with. It sets out the thinking associated with the session and the social importance of what is being learnt, the tasks and jobs that need to be completed as part of the session. As well as helping the students, this job aid was also there to keep all the adults in the room focused on what is required.

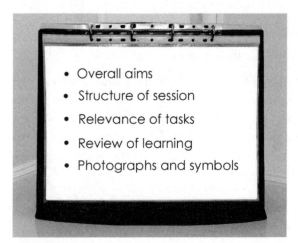

Figure 7.1 The Big Book

Personal organiser

The personal planner/organiser (see Figure 7.2) is essentially an information processing system. It is also a shared tool that staff can use to say, 'I don't know – let's look in your organiser' and then look together to find things out. In addition to the information that was produced and shared by all students, there were some who needed additional, visual support systems, presented in a simple, graphic form. It is a 'book of knowledge' of the strategies that will help each *individual* create a profile of himself. The personal organiser contains:

- Timetable.
- School rules/reminders of school systems.
- Plans for calming (see Chapter 9).
- Plans to be with people.
- Plans to ask for help.
- Rewards.

The organiser is set up at the beginning of the term, although the daily timetable might change in the course of a term.

Figure 7.2 The personal organiser

At the start of a session the students would look at their timetable to find out the following:

- What the task/job is.
- Where the job/task is to be completed.
- Who will be there to help.
- The individual steps (see the task instruction sheet, Figure 7.3).

- How the student will know when the task is finished.

- What the student will do on completion of the task.

- What the reward will be for the completion of the task (this could be sticker charts towards an agreed reward system for the individual).

Making children familiar with their thinking and ideas invites children to find solutions for any difficulties. The particular focus of the organiser depended upon what was important to the student. It was designed in a personalised way for each student. Looking at the timetable is a key time when the adult discusses with the students their view of the task and how compatible this is with their current state/mood. (Do they see the task as easy/hard and do they need an immediate reward or just points towards a delayed reward?) The timetable is used as a toolkit to find out what is appropriate on that day in that session, and what would work for the individual.

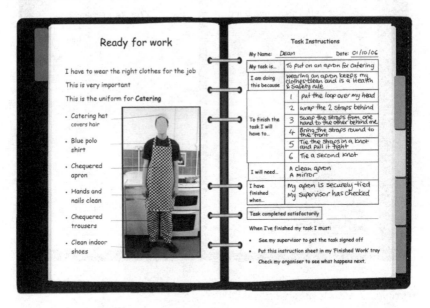

Figure 7.3 The task instruction sheet

So the organiser encourages students to:

- search for and store information systematically

- select the relevant information

- remember

- imagine what to do next.

The organiser can take any form, but it should be a portable tool in order that children can continue to learn away from school. It is essential that as many adults as possible including parents and carers are convinced of the value of using a toolkit of ideas that will help to develop the children as independent thinkers. Students who have left Risinghill have reflected on how they use a diary in adult life in a similar way to their use of the organiser at school.

Flip-charts

Figure 7.4 Flip-chart

Flip-charts (see Figure 7.4) were used at Risinghill as another tool for a shared exploration between the adult and the student(s). They could be used flexibly and carried to different settings as reminders to help students. They were often used in situations when something had happened that had not been planned for, such as exploring good ideas, noting ideas that needed to be returned to at the end of a session and also for problem solving or debriefing with individual students. The writing or drawing created a way of thinking about different perspectives and alternatives. This is an extension for thinking and showing that you value different ideas. The adult can present the concepts of:

- What can we do – what else can we try?
- What is the alternative?

- What choices do we have?

- What are the plus/minus/interesting facts?

- What are the easy/hard/never tried before ideas?

The sympathetic adult helps to explain differences in thinking and where things might have gone wrong. This procedure models an approach to 'failure' as a stage in thinking about how something went wrong but that now we need to think about how to fix the situation. We can encourage honesty about 'problems' by using phrases such as:

- I didn't know that.

- Can you help me understand?

- I'm thinking this because...

We found mind-mapping to be a useful tool to share different students' thoughts about a forthcoming activity. For example, 'We are going to the shop, what are you thinking?' The mind-mapping would help the students to prepare for a task and to take on board the different activities that they will be engaging when out in public. So, for example, if the mind-mapping shows that there is one student who is obsessed about getting his comic and experience has shown that he might run off to get the comic from a shop, then planning with him before he left would help to prepare the support tactics that would be needed on the trip. In this way we could be proactive in planning how to support the student rather just being reactive. From the students' point of view they learnt over time that flip-charts were a way of preventing problems and planning how to overcome stressful and challenging situations (see Figure 7.5).

Graphic support cards

Throughout the day at Risinghill we used a range of cards with simple graphics or short phrases/mantras (see Figure 7.6). These were often used as a job aid for staff to remind the students of rules at times when it was not easy to display a visual system. They were frequently held as small, laminated cards on a key ring or in a wallet and used as a reminder for the student to ask for help or to request anything that will help his thinking, in a way that adults are likely to respond to constructively. They could be used to ask the student, 'Do you need help?', 'Do you need a break?' or 'Do you need a massage?' In other words, they were used as a prompt to find out what the student might need.

Figure 7.5 Mind-mapping

All of our lives are full of visual supports but what was special about the graphic support cards was their use by adults to encourage the students to think about what would help them wherever they were. Adults need to respect and to acknowledge the importance of visual communication in helping students with ASD, to help them make sense of what they need to do, for example, 'Queue here', 'Wash your hands now.' Staff need to point out these graphics all around the school and in local communities, in order to help the children to realise that graphics are everywhere and for everyone.

Figure 7.6 Graphic support cards

Task instruction sheets

At Risinghill we aimed for students to complete tasks independently using a task instruction sheet (see Figure 7.3). The sheets set out the following:

- What the task is.

- Where the task is to be completed.

- Who will be available to help (and do they need visual support to ask for help)?

- Step-by-step breakdown of the job (based on student assessment and task analysis).

- When we will know the job is finished.

- What the student will do on completion of the job.

- What the reward will be for completion of the session.

Staff were trained in the use of task instruction sheets when learning about task analysis methods as a part of the LEAD course (see Chapter 10).

Wall charts

The school would have on display current topics that the group were rehearsing (see Figures 7.7 and 7.8). This might be practising how to go into a room where there is a meeting.

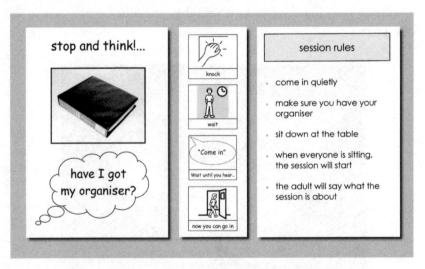

Figure 7.7 From a student's organiser and also enlarged wall chart on display in the classroom

The group may be working on relatedness and thinking how to develop personalised strategies for asking for help.

Figure 7.8 From a student's organiser

Wall charts were also used to remind the group of the class rules and expectations. For example:

- Come into the room.

- Get your organiser.

- Sit at the table.

- The adult will talk about the next session when everyone is sitting.

All these visualisation tools give a repeatable structure and provide a focus. This was part of how we communicated always and wherever we were. All of these visual supports were portable and available throughout the school site. It was crucial that all of the staff were trained in and confident with the various visual systems described above so that the students could benefit from seeing the adults demonstrate confidently how useful these approaches were for them. Used together the various systems make clear what is to be done, why and what end result is achieved. The use of visual support systems was fundamental to how we communicated and how we explained ideas to the young people. Importantly, it also encouraged the staff to restrict spoken communications. The visual supports helped the adults to keep the pace of the session appropriate, to keep the language positive and to provide supports tailored to individuals. What was of particular help to the students was that the visual supports have a lasting impact and act as a permanent reminder as opposed to the fleeting nature of spoken communications. These visual systems also proved very useful for staff in terms of how they conducted their own work – in meetings, in planning the week and in making strategic curriculum developments.

Chapter 8

RELATIONSHIP TECHNIQUES – DEVELOPING A REFLECTIVE SELF

As we have stressed many times, the approach developed at Risinghill emphasised a helping, problem-solving relationship with students rather than a directive, didactic relationship (although there was of course plenty of direct instruction as well). The broad aims were to enhance students' well-being and positive social functioning. However, within these broad aims we were keen to develop self-awareness, to help students monitor their internal world, communicate about that and self-regulate when possible. Research on autism tends to emphasise the difficulties that people on the spectrum have with understanding the outside world, particularly the social world. From our perspective as practitioners there is as great a difficulty with understanding the internal world, with 'knowing yourself', with monitoring feelings, thoughts and other internal states and dealing with internal difficulties that can arise.

The simple practices that were used drew upon two streams of psychology. The first was developmental psychology – the parenting practices that promote self-regulation. These include ongoing dialogue about the inner workings of people and the use of explanations alongside rules, rewards and punishments. The second stream was that of the Rogerian tradition in counselling, with its emphasis on careful questioning, active listening and reflecting back as the means of developing insight and assisting with problem solving.

These ideas informed the general style we adopted (see Chapter 6) and many informal encounters with students. There were also specific interactions that were structured to promote the outcomes that we are considering here.

Reflecting on events

As much as possible staff made time to discuss their sessions with the students. The plenary in the lesson was more than just a summing up of what happened, but a way of helping the students to think about what went on in the lesson and reflect back. The staff would ask:

- What helped?

- What do we need to do differently next time?

- What did staff say/do that let you know that you were doing a good job?

- What did that feel like?

Notable events would be considered in more detail. The method of using flip-charts to help understand a particular incident/event (see Chapter 5) included staff using a pictorial representation of what had happened from the students' perspective. The drawings helped to create a mind-map for the children so that they could understand different perspectives and why another student may have responded in a certain way. This technique helped students to see that events may have happened because others did not understand. It reinforced the more general notion that events have causes because many students with ASD struggle with this kind of cause–effect thinking. As a part of this flip-chart session with the students we aimed to help them develop a plan to make things better in future, to see how understanding links up with practical action. For example, 'My autism makes it hard to listen to high voices,' 'Staff need to understand that I find it hard when things don't run to time.' As well as encouraging the growth of self-awareness, these sessions could lead to practical changes such as staff adapting aspects of the curriculum delivery (for instance, timetabling tea between a 15-minute period rather than at a specific time).

Notable events would include difficult or distressed behaviour. For instance, if a student appeared upset a staff member would ask, 'What's wrong?' and suggest, 'Draw me a picture so that I can understand' or 'Can you draw it for me?' The students used small white marker boards (A5 size) on which they would draw simple pictures to show what was going on for them. For instance:

- It was too noisy.

- I felt hot.

- Too many words were being used.

- Waiting was hard.

Again, self-awareness was linked to practical action. As a result of this direct feedback from students about what was going on for them, the school taught specific strategies to deal with certain situations – for example to take deep breaths or count backwards from ten when waiting.

Reflecting on personal states

Reflecting on events of course included reflecting on how the student thought and felt about things. Also there were additional specific ways in which awareness of internal states was promoted.

As a part of an acceptance that students experienced physical reactions to difficult situations staff would ask, 'Where does it feel?' to which students might point to their head, or even say that, 'My head feels fuzzy.' The staff would hold a flat hand against their chest asking, 'Was it here? Did you feel your heart pounding?' Or with a flat hand on the stomach, to which younger students might respond, 'My tummy feels funny' or older ones might say, 'My gut's churning.' Staff would then try to help students understand typical physical reactions to feelings of fright, flight or fight. We developed a particular way of getting students to think about how they were feeling before the session started and whether they felt ready for this learning. We used the terms 'silly head' or 'sensible head' as a way of representing this without overemphasising an evaluative element of 'good' and 'bad'. Linked to this work was a communicative routine. One of the key communicative skills that the school fostered with the students was the ability and means to ask for help. Asking for help relies upon students knowing when they need help. The school used *I'm OK/I need help* cards, with one phrase on either side. This helped the students to develop their sense of self, to show *I'm OK* when they feel fine, to develop a sense of relationship and to ask for help when needed.

These issues were also addressed through some of the more general techniques that formed part of the 'Risinghill way'.

Mantras

These were set phrases used across the school and over the years. They were put in place in order to achieve consistency in communication by different staff with students. They also helped staff to understand their role in developing an effective, helping relationship with students and to give clear signals to students about the role of staff. This role is not about being friendly, but setting out clearly the rules and expectations while remaining at all times helpful. Some of these mantras emphasised self-awareness. They were reminders to check in with yourself and to think. For example:

- This is serious.

- Is something wrong? How can I help?

- Sometimes things go wrong.

- Can we make a plan?

- Can we draw a picture to explain what's happening?

- Check your organiser; can you use your calm plan to help?

Choice making

Making choices should require the student to reflect upon personal states and social understanding before acting. However, this does not necessarily happen and choice making can be 'impulsive'. So choice making has to be structured if it is to be a vehicle for encouraging self-awareness. One way that was used for doing this was in relation to planning learning. The approach that staff were trained in was to use task analysis and then to plan with the student which parts of the task they could achieve independently and which they would need help with (such as through physical, gestural or verbal prompts). This decision making involved specific elements and set phrases to encourage self and social awareness in the process:

- You come to Risinghill to learn to work.

- Sometimes your autism makes it difficult for you to do certain things.

- Your choices are that if you find things difficult you can:

  ○ work alone

  ○ work in a quiet space

  ○ have someone to work alongside you to complete the task.

- What are your choices here?

The techniques we describe are hardly novel. Nor did they produce great moments of insight and sudden shifts in personal functioning. But their relentless implementation over the years did, we believe, yield significant improvements in self-awareness and self-regulation for our students. These are important expectations for us to retain. Although Theory of Mind research has illuminated some of the difficulties that some people, including those on the autistic spectrum, experience, its implications are sometimes quite negative and limiting (as when others use such absolute terms as 'mind blindness' to refer to the difficulties that people on the spectrum have). It also emphasises the primacy of understanding others over understanding yourself. It was important for us to challenge any such limiting expectations and to find and implement practices that we believed would yield greater understanding of both the self and others alongside the more direct work to enhance behavioural aspects of personal functioning.

Chapter 9

RELATIONSHIP TECHNIQUES –
BODY BASICS AND MASSAGE

The beginning

When we first worked with this group of students there was little written about effective treatments or activities for managing anxiety and helping students gain a sense of relaxation and well-being. We understood about autism and the importance of staff as emotionally stable adults able to support stress regulation, but had not developed the approaches that we would later incorporate into all activities and use regularly throughout the day.

The importance of relationships

Developing shared relationships with students soon became a key element in our curriculum. We saw emotional regulation as intimately bound up with an ongoing, working relationship. We began by helping staff to think about the unintended messages that they gave to students if they did not feel a natural warmth towards them. We also acknowledged that if staff had difficult personal issues to deal with, that these should not get in the way of their communications with the students, but should be parked at the school gates. Indeed the important thing was for all the staff to see the good qualities in each individual child and to communicate messages about these in a genuine way. Rather than saying, 'Well done' or 'Good work' we would elaborate so that the student understood the link between what he did and our response (for example, 'Well done, I really liked the way you remembered to knock on the door'). We did not allow some of the current thinking at the time about students with ASD needing a greater personal space to become a barrier to us getting in close and building relationships. The use of structure, including the physical, gestural and verbal prompting (derived from the EDY principles mentioned in Chapter 5) as well as the graphics and mantras ensured that students experienced a relationship with an adult where the emotional connection was made explicit. These relationships were seen as helping students to engage in the style of learning and community that we were creating in school.

Overcoming anxiety and fight and flight reactions

Many of our students had already learnt unsuccessful survival strategies. We observed that in structured situations, significant numbers of students demonstrated unexplained mood swings that resulted in confrontational or impulsive behaviours or a withdrawal from contact with the activity or adult. As educators one of our major concerns is when children take 'flight' or demonstrate complete withdrawal and are unable to return to the learning task. As mentioned in Chapter 2, before coming to Risinghill, most of the students had unsuccessful experiences in secondary schools during which many developed the strategy of wandering around to escape from the difficulties of being in the classroom. At Risinghill we believed in the approach of tackling how they felt. This involved getting them to:

- think about how they felt, both emotionally and physically

- learn how feelings were triggered

- understand that feelings could vary in magnitude

- learn how they could influence or regulate those feelings.

The strategies

The students seemed uncomfortable and 'out of touch' with their bodies. On a daily basis students looked tired and tense, with backs rigid and shoulders tight. When something went wrong some students would clench their fists and leer threateningly towards you, looking you directly in the face. You could see their breathing changing, faces reddening, and signs of perspiration forming. Others, fewer in number, became more rigid and withdrawn, typically with shoulders hunched, backs rounded, choosing to sink into their chairs or lean against a wall in order to avert eye gaze. These students also manifested high levels of tension in their bodies. These off task or out of control behaviours were initially interpreted as a form of communication, representing the student's level of insecurity. However, we were concerned that if we allowed students to use anxiety driven behaviours to communicate when things were going wrong then we were limiting the ways in which they would be able to initiate a positive response from supporting adults.

The staff approach to this range of physical responses was not to label this as being part of autism but to develop both our and the students' understanding of their bodies and to see the links between triggers in the environment and their physical reactions associated with a range of emotions. As part of the curriculum delivery we wanted to incorporate tactile and kinaesthetic learning approaches into our style of working. This was based on our understanding of the importance of touch and movement to emotional well-being. Brain research tells us that positive touch is essential because of its role in regulating strong emotional feelings. Any nurturing contact helps to mitigate strong emotional reactions and provides a measure of positive support when we are highly stressed or anxious. The students' tactile sense provides a reality check, so that when they are reassured by a warm palm on the back of their hand, combined with a message from the adult saying, 'I'm here to help, I'm here, you're OK now' – the physical contact helps in the development of the feeling of 'I'm OK'.

Autism and touch

Some people with ASD are described as 'untouchable' or 'touchy'. Some are described as 'tact-less' because they are unable to appreciate when they use 'hurtful' words. Some children with ASD have sensory modulation issues and are described as touch sensitive or touch defensive and when this happens touch registered by the skin becomes a warning system for the primitive reflexes of flight or fight. In all of these situations the heart rate increases, whether a student runs out of the classroom, stays and confronts the teacher, or even sometimes when the child appears to 'withdraw' but may be feeling quite anxious while apparently in a passive state. The heart beats faster, breathing becomes shallow, muscles tense and tighten, and thinking becomes difficult. When the body systems are continually out of balance, due to high levels of anxiety, irregularities develop in eating, digestion and sleep patterns, making children feel unwell. The adrenal glands secrete adrenalin which causes further loss of emotional control and we lose the ability to use any previously successful self-calming or self-occupation strategies.

At times it was apparent that there were extremes of distress or frustration. We noticed this through the way in which the students would self-injure by body slamming against an object, punching their faces, slapping their heads, or pulling their hair. Quite a few of the older students picked at their skin and nails or made marks with sharp objects. A small cut would be picked until it bled again. The inability of the students to self-calm constructively, but rather to present maladaptive physical responses needed to be tackled with a different approach.

A different approach

Well-being training (with John Clements) emphasised the importance of recognising the intense feelings associated with anxiety and led to the development specific activities that would support or alleviate symptoms of anxiety. Initially this started with the creation of books that represented the positive activities the students engaged in and liked doing. This was linked with developing appropriate language, 'You look calm and relaxed,' 'You look as if you are thinking,' and 'You look like you're having a good time.' The focus on positive feelings was to facilitate exploration of this whole area. Starting with negative feelings would have been more difficult as from the students' point of view such feelings had often been associated with behaviour difficulties for which they had been criticised.

In order for students to be self-reliant and learn to make appropriate responses, we needed to help them recognise that their internal feelings and external behaviours could be an indicator that something was going wrong with the body's ability to cope with a new or stressful situation. We were sympathetic when students complained of headache or backache and linked this to signs of possible stress or physical need. We built in regular time for snack rewards that did not have to be earned in order to keep hydration and blood sugar levels high and to directly inhibit anxiety. At all times we showed students ways of massaging their necks or backs to alleviate some of the tension and discovered that significant numbers of children had incredibly tight neck or shoulder muscles.

Students were taught the physical sensations that arise from arousal, such as changes to heart rate, increased rate of breathing, increased heat or temperature in their heads or hands, and perspiration levels. This was done by increasing the level of aerobic activities in the timetable, which was not just once or twice a week but interspersed throughout the day and introduced particularly at times when students had been sitting for a while. These included classroom games such as row the boat, or stir the pudding, and playground games such as jumping jacks and hopping quickly. Walking at a fast pace, then a slow pace was used to show how quickly the heart rate and breathing could accelerate and then return to a more comfortable level. It emphasised the controllability of these phenomena.

Frequent practice at staff meetings as well as at in-service training days helped to develop consistency across the curriculum. New games were created for use at the start and end of sessions. We called these the 'let's pre-vent' strategies, emphasising the importance of breathing to support relaxation. We paid attention to cueing the students into awareness of their bodies, by noticing the feeling of tension in the hands. We did this by making fists and pairing the word 'tight' and then opening the hands wide linking the words 'stretch and relax'. We observed that shaking of the hands was a natural consequence of holding the hands clenched and we added 'letting go' to this action. In time we introduced other activities such as squeezing down the arm with a flat hand and making small thumb circles in the palm of the hand. We called these responses for anxious moments. Staff used an exaggerated breath 'phew' or 'ahhh' to accompany the process of letting go, relaxing and decreasing tension throughout the body. Students became interested in the pressure points on the hand and used thumb pressure in the palm of the hand to feel themselves getting back into control. Another favourite was holding the forefinger in a clenched fist until you could feel a pulse rate that slowly decreased accompanied by slower breathing. It is interesting that recent developments with bio-feedback of the heart rate have been used in some educational settings, specifically to help students become aware of their own physical reactions and to bring about calm.

In a mainstream class you may observe a group of children adopting supportive poses as they listen to their teacher. They adopt postures that support containment and control. Typically their hands are relaxed and placed somewhere on their body, supporting their heads in their hands when thinking, holding their hands when listening or wrapping their arms across their body when relaxed. Very few of our children with ASD demonstrated this listening posture. They slumped, slouched forward, sat upright or paced the room.

In response to this we taught specific gestures and phrases to promote greater self-awareness, gestures which, coincidentally, all stimulate the respiratory system:

- Hands on my head help me think.
- Hands on my chest help me breathe.
- Hands on my tummy help me relax.
- Hands on my knees or in my lap show I'm in control.

Staff would model an exaggerated thinking pose with their hand on their forehead, accompanied by a thoughtful, 'Mmmm', and loud exhalation. The association of achievement was linked to calm breathing and thinking – 'I really liked the way you used your hand on your body, I could see you were thinking.'

'Breathe and blow' became a mantra for when things were getting tough. Games included:

- Breathing into the palm of the hand.

- Blowing cotton wool balls and feathers.

- Blowing across the tops of bottles to produce a deep R sound.

We emphasised the importance of staff physically modelling what we wanted students to practice through consciously shaping the beginning and the end of activities. We linked our actions with mantras, for example, 'When your heart is beating fast you need to breathe and blow' or 'Let's take three calm breaths and see what good ideas we can think about.' We believed that it was important before a child began the activities in a session that they could say and feel, 'I'm OK, I can do this.' We constantly reiterated that, 'Breathe and blow means being calm and relaxed.' Being calm and relaxed is the state you need to be in to do your best work. We introduced breathing games, based on the length of exhalation, rather than holding the breath. For example:

- Breathing out to the count of 4, 6, 12 and 16.

- Tarzan breath, pounding the chest, holding the 'aaaah' for as long as possible.

- Blowing out real or imaginary candles.

In child development the warmth and support of the care-giver is seen as essential to the development of self-regulation. This is based on the understanding that children who develop positive touch relationships become more assured about themselves and more self-confident. The profile of our students identified that these early developmental stages may not have been experienced in pre-school settings, where the dominance of their autism meant that students were isolated and withdrawn, cut off from these kinds of inputs and left to spend large periods of time engaged in their own preoccupations. Touching and being touched is part of the turn taking, giving and receiving that takes place during play. Our emotional development is partly based on the experience of our own skin, knowing what feels good is part of our developing self-awareness. This initial nurturing that takes place between care-giver and the child creates a relationship of trust which can be re-created through a range of positive physical activities within school.

Massage was introduced with the specific intention of encouraging and supporting students in being able to relax and let go of tension held in their muscles. This was introduced through the training of all staff in the use of massage and maintained through weekly staff meetings in which staff showed a massage story (see Figure 9.1) that they had developed for use with the students as well as the way they had been used with a colleague. We called our massage programme 'Touchtalks', and our approach supported sensory processing, helping children perceive, organise and process words through their kinaesthetic system. One of the aims of using massage stories was to revisit earlier stages of development where stories and rhymes have a tactile component, for example, 'Incy wincy spider climbing up the spout', or 'Round and round the garden like a teddy bear'. As well as their physical and emotional impact these shared activities build social communication skills and provide conversational practice in turn taking, following a sequence of speaker and listener, giver and receiver.

Positive touch and massage protocol

The successful use of massage at Risinghill was written up into an accredited course, approved by the Guild of Infant and Child Massage and the International Federation of Aromatherapists as an NVQ Level 2 course. Within the policy it was made clear that staff would be fully trained in order to undertake massage with students. It also indicated that parent and student permission was necessary and that parents were to be provided with written information about massage, as well as invited to attend training alongside staff. It was also made clear for the pupils where it was acceptable to touch and not to touch. Anywhere covered by a swimming costume was a private area. In addition we added a physical routine demonstrating that where your arms crossed in front or behind your body was personal space and a private place. Asking permission to touch was always the starting point: 'Can I massage your back, can I tell you a back story?' An information sheet in the Big Book identified the part of the body to be touched, the words and the massage strokes to be used. Students were introduced to the strokes by using names that were relevant to their understanding such as circle, hearts, lines, waves. Other strokes were linked to activities like the weather, sunrays, clouds, rain, hailstones. Students identified that a flat hand and firm pressure was preferable to lighter movements.

Initially each story was written specifically for an individual student reflecting something that had happened during their day, but gradually group stories were introduced and sessions developed into peer massage activities. Students had cards to be used to request time out from an activity or time with an adult for a massage. Over time we saw a decrease in the amount of time children took themselves out of the classroom and an increase in requests for a massage. A massage story became the preferred activity for staff to finish a lesson.

The Pizza Story

You can be standing or sitting, facing your partner's back.

We're making a pizza
Pretend to roll out the dough with a flat hand starting in the middle of the back.

Spreading tomato paste
Pretend to spread the paste using a flat hand, starting from the shoulders work left to right until you reach the belt line and stop.

Adding the cheese
Keep your hands flat and apply pressure through the fingers to make small grating movement.

What shall we add?
Ask your partner. Draw the shape of the food they choose.

Pineapple – chopped or rings?

Sliced pepperoni?

Olives!
Make sure you make big movements with a flat hand.

Put it in the oven
Draw a clock face counting slowly from 1–12.

Mmmm, smells delicious – it's hot!
Make an exaggerated sound and blow out to cool the pizza.

Cut it into slices
This is a slow movement as you say finish, finish, finish and sigh, 'mmmm!'

Figure 9.1 An example of a massage story

As students responded to touch, it became possible to use a more nurturing style of touch on the back or arm, both as a prompt to breathe and relax and an acknowledgement of self-control. This reflected warmth in the relationship demonstrating not only the students' awareness of self, but also their awareness of others. In child development this physical feeling that someone cares for you, leads to secure attachment and can contribute as a building block for emotional and social adjustment. In time we opened a well-being clinic at the school and students could book a session of back, foot or hand massage, recognising that this could be a choice they might make as adults.

All the strategies used were contained in the first pages of the student organiser, identified as plans to calm. It suggested the range of options that would support difficult times as well as the identified places that students could go, for a fixed time, without being interrupted by an adult. Some students preferred their own personalised system of photographs rather than graphics, reflecting a stronger sense of 'this is me'.

All well-being activities were supported by image work presented in the Big Book. We were aware that students needed ongoing support and help in identifying thoughts that go with new and potentially stressful situations, for example, 'This is a new job or a hard job, so I need to breathe and blow.' It was rewarding to see students reach the phase when they identified, 'This is an easy job, I'm in control' or use an information card – 'This is hard, I need a break – I'll be back in five minutes.'

The use of these approaches to promote well-being was a very visible part of the curriculum. The sessions took place in classrooms or the gym, and all the adults in the room participated. Parents were also given training in massage techniques so that when their children indicated that the strategy worked and they wanted massage at home the parents could provide this.

Evaluation of the work

The impact of the use of massage was evaluated by Julia Hardy as a part of her work as educational psychologist at Risinghill. Using an action research model the students responded to a structured questionnaire about how the use of massage stories at school helped with their well-being. Pupils aged between 9 and 16 gave their views. The majority felt that having a massage made them feel happy or very happy and the majority indicated that they had, or would like to have massage at home. The most common emotion that they described feeling as a result of massage was being calm and many of the students found massage to be helpful after they had been feeling angry or upset.

Concluding remarks

The approach at Risinghill saw the development of emotional regulation and the promotion of positive well-being as central areas of concern. It was understood that this work needed to be carried on day in, day out, and be woven into the fabric of everyday life and interaction. It was not about having 'lessons' on emotions or doing 'ten sessions of anger management training'. It was a developmental approach taking place in the context of daily life rather than 'therapy'.

One of the greatest dangers of implementing a new approach is giving up too soon. Introducing these new strategies to promote well-being through the use of Body Basics and massage needed thought given to making it embedded into the school day. The new and somewhat different ideas needed to be accepted by staff. The approaches had to be practised on a daily basis for a considerable time before positive effects could be seen. Choosing the best approach for each student required trialling and assessment then a review as to whether the planned strategies for each individual needed to be updated. Things needed to move on as development occurred but the central concept remained unchanged, that learning to calm was a key area of work for each student and a vital part of building longer term resilience for our students. (See Appendix 2 for an interesting research finding related to the work described in this chapter.)

Chapter 10

RELATIONSHIP TECHNIQUES – REWARD, PUNISHMENT AND A CULTURE OF CELEBRATION

Consequences are rightly viewed as an important vehicle for effecting change in human behaviour. They can impact on behaviour in a number of ways (see below). Some of these impacts – the processes of reinforcement and punishment – involve technical considerations around immediacy and consistency and these technical matters often dominate any discussion of consequences. However, from the point of view of this book such a technical discussion is not enough and we would want to locate consequences in a broader social context.

Consequences and context

The technical view of consequences suggests that as long as a programme is technically sound it will be effective no matter who delivers that programme and in what context. This is not a view to which this book subscribes. It is the belief of the authors that context matters hugely, that the effectiveness of consequences is influenced by both who is delivering the programme and by the broader social environment.

In particular we would draw attention to the importance of the kinds of relationships that we have described earlier – empathic, clear, strong and consistent, with a definite attitude of wanting to help and an overarching belief in the positive potential of our students. We would draw attention to elements of the organisational culture, a culture focused on:

- problem solving

- a belief in our ability to solve whatever problems came our way

- the importance of celebrating success

- the importance of a commitment to make information as clear as possible so that understanding could increase over time.

We wanted our students not only to change their behaviour, but to:

- grow in knowledge and understanding

- feel more positive in and about themselves

- be more motivated by learning.

It would be our contention that embedding specific programmes of behaviour change by consequences in this broader context made it much more likely that these programmes would have an impact than if they were delivered on a stand alone basis. However, the notion of impact itself needs to be examined more closely as consequences can be used for a range of purposes.

The functions of consequences

Consequences are often described in terms of negative and positive, reinforcement and punishment, rewards and costs, carrots and sticks. They are seen as a vehicle for short-term change in behaviour – making a behaviour more likely (reinforcement) or less likely (punishment).

However, consequences can serve other important psychological purposes:

1. They may contribute to cognitive change by providing feedback that says 'this is what is wanted' – they can provide a clear signpost, especially important for people whose access to understanding by traditional routes (having things explained) is impaired in some way.

2. Consequences can also impact emotionally, leading to those experiencing them feeling good or bad both within and about themselves.

3. There is an additional impact of negative consequences where the consequence involves the separation of those involved in the conflict. Here the consequence may lead to the calming of negative emotions and the return to a more stable emotional state.

4. Consequences can serve a social function – they are a way of demonstrating what a group values, that if you want to be a valued member of this group, this is what you need to do. This impact is on the motivation and commitment of those who observe the consequences not just on those who receive them directly.

5. Consequences, especially negative consequences, can have a bureaucratic function – they can be applied in line with an agreed disciplinary procedure which can then lead to the permanent exclusion of the individual from the environment in which the behaviour occurred.

Thus when we discuss consequences at Risinghill we are looking at a range of interventions that serve a number of functions. Most importantly we are locating these interventions in a broader social context, as a part of our way of communicating with and supporting our students.

Consequences at Risinghill

The majority of students at Risinghill had been excluded from their previous school(s), often spending considerable time at home before being placed. Others had been taught separately, supported by individual support staff and often withdrawn from class groups. In many instances a teaching assistant had been allocated to them, with a result that the subject/class teachers did not see it necessary to work on developing a relationship with the pupil with ASD. Therefore, when new students started at Risinghill staff were aware that there had previously been significant failures in terms of opportunities to relate successfully in an educational context. The students themselves were angry, hostile and hope-less. It was essential right from the start to communicate messages of value, possibility and hope without concealing the difficulties that would be faced or the rules that would be applied.

Positive messages and a problem-solving approach

The messages that the school gave to young people and their parents started with the interview process. This acknowledged that children came to us because of their diagnosis of autism and that this would have contributed to their previous difficulties. The school would explore:

- What went wrong at your last school?

- What did you do that made teachers annoyed?

- What helped you?

- How did you know you were doing well?

This discussion gave the school initial ideas about what we could do (such as make a graphic for the student to use saying, 'It's too noisy') or the way in which the school could use the mantra, 'It's not OK' in the case of

aggression to others. At the end of the interview days, the school gave the
student an outline of the issues discussed, illustrated in thought bubbles
and a visual representation of how things worked at Risinghill.

From early on we aimed to involve parents in supporting the process of
change, and treated them as practitioners not as clients. In parent training
we used video clips to share successful tasks and interactions at school
and then discussed with them what could be achieved at home. We found
that many parents were using the offer of a long-term reward as a way of
motivating their children. We spent time with parents in these sessions
discussing the importance of short-term, immediate and varied rewards.
We also helped parents to think about developing a culture of celebrating
achievements (however small) at home, and giving time to making a 'big
deal' of things that went well, and genuinely showing that they were
pleased. We helped them to see that it was possible to raise expectations
at home – for example, that it was quite possible for the young person to
help at home or to come to the table at meal times.

The staff at the school were clear about the purpose of their interactions
with students. Through training they were clear that they were there to
teach and to overcome difficulties that were arising from the autism.
They were empathic in their understanding of autism rather than simply
sympathetic. They would challenge an older student's response that, 'I
can't help it because of my autism' by developing a 'What would help
you?' strategy. In this way staff walked the fine line of acknowledging that
living with autism was a huge challenge, but that our belief was that autism
was an explanation of many things, and an excuse for nothing. Students
were encouraged to engage with the other children and to participate in
the school life at Risinghill. We would be clear that, 'These are the rules.'
For those with an obsessive-compulsive tendency we would acknowledge
their issues: for instance, 'I know you have to touch the door three times',
but we would then suggest strategies to manage this, for example by
letting the student go through the door last, after all the other pupils,
so that they could touch without getting in the way of others. Another
example was with a student who was destroying all the fire alarm notices
throughout the school. This student thought, 'I don't like being told what
to do', and felt that the notices were an example of this, combined with his
dislike of the alarm. Staff tackled this by drawing up a social story, asking
what if there were no notices, what would happen then? The school also
used the understanding gained to change the environment by producing
simple laminated, portable signs. At the same time the fundamental rule
was reasserted that, 'Damage to property is not OK.'

Security through consistency

Consistent with the school's philosophy of empowering *all staff* through training to develop their skills, a training package was developed that helped staff to take a functional approach to working with students. This taught staff to enquire what works well for a student and to offer a consistent, agreed approach based upon the unique interests of pupils. They learnt to ask themselves whether what they were teaching made sense as a relevant, useful skill and could be applied anywhere on the school site and throughout the whole day. The educational psychologist's perspective was combined with the pragmatic approach to the school's curriculum planning, which led to the development of a whole training package, with a focus on autism and learning methods. The training entitled Learning Environment for Autistic Development (LEAD) was very much influenced by the Hester Adrian Centre's Education of the Developmentally Young (EDY) course and mixed direct instruction with Bruner's principle of iconic (video examples) and enactive (through role play and practice with the pupil) elements. The course covered the following sessions:

- *An introduction to autism* – for new staff to understand ASD and in particular Asperger's syndrome.

- *Seeing is believing* – focusing on the differences in the ways in which students with ASD communicate, how to achieve functional understanding and the crucial importance of visual communication.

- *Teaching and LEAD* – understanding the behavioural factors in the school setting.

- *Tasks for learning* – setting 'smart' objectives, overcoming barriers to learning and collecting baseline data.

- *Using rewards to make connections* – understanding the importance of reward assessment to plan what motivates each individual, including consideration of age appropriateness and ways of negotiating and delivering rewards within a school context.

- *Helping to learn* – how to give appropriate help, including the use of physical, gestural, verbal and visual prompts.

- *Steps to success* – clarifying what a target behaviour would be and then trying out various methods of task analysis, first in theory and then through role play and finally with the student.

- *Leading the learning* – further practice of task analysis including forward and backward chaining.

- *I can do it* – in which all the previous taught elements are integrated with each member of staff planning and implementing a new learnt activity in full with a student. These various, successful activities were video-taped and shared with staff and students.

- *The final session* – here the staff on the course were assessed in the new knowledge and practice that they had learnt during the LEAD course.

In each session on the LEAD course there was a small amount of time spent covering the theory, with 75 per cent of the session focusing on how the theory could be applied in practice to work with all the students. The LEAD course was delivered to all new staff irrespective of their role and function in the school, ensuring that there was consistency and stability of staff responses.

Of course consistency is an ideal and in the real world things can go wrong. There are times when a teacher is feeling emotionally exhausted and needs someone else to take over, and continue with the same approach, without the staff member feeling that another colleague has over-ridden or contradicted what she was doing. Since all staff had the same, comprehensive training about approaches to teaching and learning, other staff could then easily go in, look at the lesson plan in the Big Book and the individual student's task instruction sheets, and take over smoothly. This consistency of approach in turn increased the children's confidence through knowing what happens with regard to school routines and what the consequences would be if they broke the school rules. Staff had available simple, laminated cards showing the school rules (see Figure 10.1). These visual reminders of school expectations were helpful both for students with literacy difficulties, but also for students in heightened arousal or anger who are less likely to attend to the words than the graphics.

The whole process is BERIS orientated (see Chapter 5): What does your body need – drink, rest, calm place, safe haven? This system was explicit both in the student handbook and in describing for staff in their induction, the tools of the trade – setting out clearly this is what staff will use.

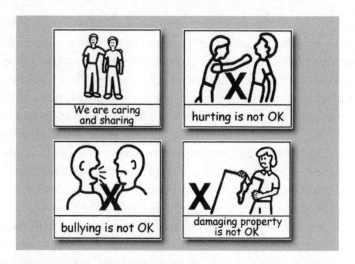

Figure 10.1 Laminated cards showing school rules

A culture of celebration

Built into the Risinghill school ethos was the culture of celebration, which was evident throughout the whole day, as well as during certain events (whole school assemblies and sharing events with parents). This culture of celebration was apparent through pre-prepared materials, such as the following:

- Certificates.

- Quick notes home.

- Positive memos.

- 'You earned it' coupons.

The staff were encouraged to increase the use of touch as a consequence, for example through hand shakes or patting students on the back when they had achieved something. The school became aware that over time there was a gradual shift from students being motivated by extrinsic (external) rewards to intrinsic (internal) ones. Initially staff were trained in planning for the students individually, through reward sampling, in order to find out what worked for each student. There was then a gradual change from giving rewards immediately after a successful task/behaviour to the use of a points system both for new learning related to individual targets or for whole class behaviour. Students liked receiving stickers, which were exchanged for points. The students then chose particular things of interest (rewards) at the end of the week that were equivalent to a number of points. Some of the students shifted from working to get things for themselves to selecting items as presents for family members. As staff became more confident in thinking about ways of motivating the students they developed whole class special experiences to reflect that the whole class had achieved things together. These included small treats at the end of the week and a bigger event, such as a special outing, at the end of each term. It is important to note that the starting point for reward schemes was simple and basic even though in many ways our students might have been regarded as 'too sophisticated' for such approaches. This chimes with our more general understanding that people are often misled by articulate students into overestimating their real needs and level of operation. In this work you may have to learn to work simultaneously with the angry teenager and the stroppy toddler. It was exciting that our students were able to move forward to much more delayed and indirect rewards, but had we started at that level our schemes would have failed to impact their behavioural functioning and general self-esteem.

More indirect consequences were also exploited. Loud whispers that the students could overhear between staff, saying, 'Did you know that…has done…' was all part of building the culture of encouragement. This helped students to see that staff would talk about things they had achieved and that this would build their reputation for positive success. This approach was achieved through the regular staff training which encouraged adults to be both natural and enthusiastic in giving praise and encouragement to students. Many staff needed opportunities to practise giving praise in a more exaggerated and attention-getting way than the normal, reserved, English manner. The language used was explicit in stating what the student did, and where and whether they achieved this on their own.

Trust developing
The change in behaviour as a result of staff setting clear boundaries and giving rewards led to a student group who had more self-control. This enabled the senior managers to design more realistic learning opportunities throughout the whole school environment to achieve 'real world learning'. For instance, students had jobs where they could walk around the site independently, being trusted to collect equipment themselves (rather than being escorted) as well as opportunities to participate in higher risk, but motivating activities such as the following:

- Driving a tractor.
- Using a leaf blower.

- Cooking in the main kitchen.
- Going off site to purchase equipment with an adult.

With the older students there was a gradual change in the relationships between staff and students, so that staff knew that students could be trusted to follow their task instruction sheet without help. Students would deliver fruit to other classes or collect items from the food store. This also enabled the school to create new titles for the students such as work assistant and site assistant.

There were evident changes in the messages given to the students that ran in parallel with the increased responsibility and trust. Initially when the adult was in charge they would use a key ring card (see Figure 10.2).

Figure 10.2 Key ring cards

This moved on to the use of the sheet in a student's organiser (see Figure 10.3).

In order to develop independence, students would have in their organiser a range of ways to choose to calm, that helped them to avoid breaking the school rule of damaging equipment.

In one sense the staff had developed confidence in handing over the control to the students, but this was a mutual experience because the students were now more motivated to undertake activities independently, while retaining their knowledge of what the consequences were if things went wrong.

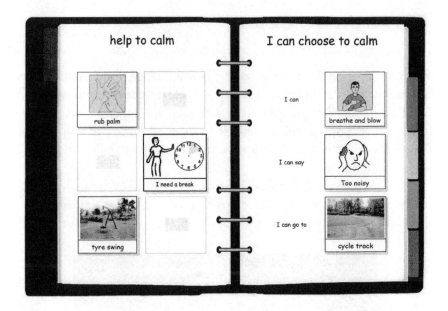

Figure 10.3 Sheets in the organiser

Dealing with rule breaking

Staff at Risinghill were empowered to use a mantra developed as part of the BERIS approach to help students think about 'I have rights and responsibilities.' There were consequences if any of the three major school rules were broken (see Figure 10.1). Staff used the key ring graphic to say, 'It's not OK to... At Risinghill students are caring,' which was used if there had been bullying. There was a core script that staff would use when rules were being broken. Staff would give three warnings as follows:

1. Letting you know... Check the Big Book or organiser to remind yourself of the task.

2. How can I help/use your prompt card – I need a break... I'm reminding you, you are working to earn your points.

3. This is your final warning – check if you've got your 'silly head' or 'sensible head'.

If the behaviour had not been resolved, at this point the staff would:

- describe the behaviour: 'You're shouting'

- describe the effect on others: 'You're stopping people from working.'

Staff would then say, 'You're choosing not to think – you need to take your organiser and go to the function room' (a multipurpose room in the school).

The purpose of this final part of the consequence was to stop the behaviour recurring in the original setting, offering an opportunity for the student to calm down and go elsewhere, and then after a space of time to meet with an adult to reflect on, 'How I could do this differently next time?' The staff member would explore with the student what happened and whether there were any triggers within the environment. The school attitude was that students are responsible for their actions. Staff would use the mantra: 'Students learn to think about their actions – they learn that there are consequences to these actions.' It is our belief that in the long term the most powerful source of self-esteem does not stem from the praise of the adult but from the acquisition of competencies – to understand situations and to manage difficulties successfully. It was an underlying expectation that students would acquire these competencies while at Risinghill. Conversations with students would finish by exploring, 'How can we make this right? What do we do the next time this happens?' The use of the function room was an ending to an incident, and the discussion with the staff member would then result in making a plan for the future and looking at the resources for the support to the student, often leading to the adding of a resource within their organiser.

The whole purpose of meeting in the function room was to understand what had happened and to plan different ways forward. There is a parallel to this approach in the work place where the role of the line manager is to support, encourage and ensure compliance with company policy. The ultimate goal is to make the organisation more efficient and effective in meeting the needs of all the employees/customers/clients through a sense of shared purpose. This similarity of approach has helped the students to transition into the world of further education and work.

However, it is important to make clear that the use of consequences following rule breaking (separation to the function room and sometimes temporary suspensions from school) were not intended as direct influences over behaviour (unlike some of the practices involving positive consequences). It was not expected that such 'punishments' would bring about short-term behavioural change (in line with behavioural theory). The consequences were not immediate enough and were not necessarily aversive (though there could be an element of that in some cases). More importantly it was our clear understanding that the students we were serving would not be touched by such direct punitive behavioural interventions. They had long experience of such interventions, were quite capable of 'serving their time' and the emotional charge involved in most incidents would wipe out any potential learning from 'punishment'. Rather, these consequences were used as a vehicle to effect calming, to encourage reflection and thinking and thus to contribute to longer term, more cognitively mediated change.

Concluding remarks

Although consequences were used in a traditional behavioural way at Risinghill this was only part of the story. They were embedded in our culture and used in a variety of ways to develop core understandings about how the outside world worked and core self-beliefs in the student. They were there to give the students the competence and the confidence to find and lead the kinds of adult lives that would work for them as young adults.

Chapter 11

TRANSITION OR TRANSFORMATION?

In Chapters 2 and 3 we described the changes over time for a sample of students and staff. This was to give a practical sense of the work done and some of the things that were achieved before we went into detail about the overall regime that developed and the specific techniques that were used within that regime. Now we return to the question of evaluation – was this an effective approach to education that changed the lives of the students and staff involved or would these changes have occurred anyway, no matter what kind of education was offered? This is most certainly not a research study so there is no 'hard' comparative data. However, it is important that we make an attempt to do the best we can to judge the effectiveness of our approach. We will do this in relation to the cohort of students around whom this work originally developed. We have been able to keep in touch with these students, even after they left the school. In addition we will consider how the students' families evaluated the approach.

Did everyone succeed?

Our cohort came in at secondary level and it was our intention to take them through to the end of their time in the school system (16–19 years old, depending on circumstances). There were three children who left us before that time. In all cases this reflected home and family issues rather than anything to do with the student's behaviour. In one case the home could no longer support the student and a full-time residential placement was needed. In two other cases it proved difficult for us to forge an effective, constructive working relationship with the family. The relationship was marked by conflict and dissatisfaction and led the families to seek an alternative placement. This is not a question of blaming families but illustrates some very important facts:

- Families should have choice over where and how their child is educated and it is not to be expected that one particular approach will suit every family.

- The level of home-based support to families with very challenging children on the autistic spectrum is, with very few exceptions, dismally inadequate in the UK. Families are left caring for such challenging children with very limited support and can end up angry, frustrated, desperate and depressed. In that context it can be very difficult to forge good relationships with service providing agencies, especially as the school was not resourced to provide intensive family support services.

There was one child who was on the verge of leaving but who we switched to home-based education managed from the school (using the same approaches but in a different context). This resulted in positive developments beyond anyone's expectations, developments continuing to this day, although responsibility for the programme has now passed to another agency (for administrative reasons).

The rest of the group of 16 saw out their education with us and have now moved on in directions to be described later.

What changes occurred over time?
Students
The positive outcomes for the students were many and varied:

- The students learnt a lot of specific skills and their behavioural challenges declined in frequency and intensity to the point of not constituting a barrier to their development.

- This was accompanied by a marked growth in self-awareness and self-regulation, including the ability to ask for help when needed.

- They grew in confidence and self-esteem, taking more pride in their appearance and becoming more flexible. They could accommodate others better and play by other people's rules when needed.

- The students remain very proud of their experience and what they have achieved.

- None of their 'obsessions' changed or went away and as a group they remained people who liked to do things their own way. Nevertheless the increased flexibility and ability to accommodate others when necessary meant that such personal characteristics did not set unnecessary limits on the lives that they were able to lead.

- It was also noticeable how the students took over and used for themselves key elements of the system, particularly the use of mantras and the use of the organiser. They varied in how they did it (from using scrap bits of paper to more high-tech approaches with their computers and mobile phones) but they continued to find these things useful.

- The students most certainly grew in well-being and this has been sustained. None are currently involved with mental health services.

- In terms of life outcomes the majority of the students (nine) have moved on to college as an intermediate step to employment, so we cannot be sure how many will make it into the job market long term. However, seven are supporting themselves through work (see Chapter 2) and a lot have part-time (Saturday) jobs such as working at a pet store, being a handyman, operating a checkout. None are just retrieving trolleys at supermarkets.

- With one exception all of the students have remained living at home.

- Several of the students have learnt to drive (cars or motor cycles).

Our students have remained the people that they always were. Even so many specifics changed and, we would argue, their life prospects have been transformed.

Staff

Many staff came and went during the time considered in this book. We have not been able to keep in touch with all of them but we have been able to keep in touch with a core group who were with us for much of the time in question. In terms of their achievements:

- They too grew in confidence and felt empowered as they were able to see their work as effective and attributable to the specific techniques that they had learnt.

- In particular the staff report how much they benefited from the regular monthly peer coaching sessions in which they took turns to talk through the particular issues that they faced in their day to day work. They appreciated being trained in solution-focused methods so that they could be helped by a peer to talk through and explore in detail topics of concern within the group consultation sessions.

- They continue to use the specific practices and as a group of people are 'solution focused' as opposed to people who moan about problems without tackling them.

- Although everyone has now changed jobs they have all remained in the autism field and gone on to jobs with more responsibility.

Our staff have remained the people that they always were. However, many specifics have changed and, we would argue, their life prospects have been transformed.

It is also important to note that all the staff we are in touch with keep in contact with one or more of the students that they worked with at Risinghill. Some of the students also keep in touch with each other and some meet up as well.

The familes' perspectives

The ongoing dialogue with parents was a distinctive feature of the Risinghill style of working. An example of this is that in the last annual parents' survey the school received over 200 separate written comments about the work at the school, including many valuable ideas and suggestions. Subsequently, key themes were introduced to parents and staff at a presentation in the summer sharing, and this was a way of showing the governing body's appreciation of the school's commitment to the students.

Readiness for leaving school

Parents indicated a range of things that they felt the school was working towards their child achieving by the time they left Risinghill. Their top three aspirations were the following.

1. For their child to be better prepared to manage everyday life and able to work with others and accept instructions

With regard to the development of vocational skills, parents also commented that their child was learning functional vocational skills, which were steadily increasing in range and were being generalised for use in the home setting. The parents were pleased that the students were achieving NVQ qualifications, which helped them to learn practical skills to prepare for work; as well as gaining good enough basic literacy and numeracy skills to manage at work. The practical skills included time-keeping, handling money and being able to choose to wear appropriate clothing for the world of work. It was a combination of 'real world learning' opportunities on the school site and extended work experience that provided this.

2. For their child to learn to understand and manage his or her own autism

Feedback from parents showed that the majority of them felt the school had helped their child to become better at understanding his or her autism, and that their child was also becoming better at managing social situations and interacting. This included making friends and developing relationships with others, as well as being able to ensure that they were safe at all times and had some ability to protect themselves from the negative influences of others.

3. For their child to be able to manage his or her emotions

For parents, it was very important that their child could be helped to become better able to manage frustration and anxiety, in order to be prepared to manage everyday life and able to work with others and accept instructions.

Other aspirations

In addition to these three themes, all parents were interested in the improvement of their child's basic literacy and numeracy skills and their ability to participate in creative and physical activities, and wanted their child to be happy and helped to find the role that they wanted in adult life.

What do families say now that their child has left Risinghill and is an adult?

Five families were followed up to complete our understanding of the process of transition and transformation for their young people into adult life. Their comments give an interesting window into how families saw the changes that occurred during their children's final years at Risinghill and how these young adults are functioning now.

What was unique about Risinghill?

One family talked about the importance of their son being taught in 'small classes' at Risinghill, 'but taught in a group [as opposed to his previous experience in a secondary school of being removed, and] so he was never isolated'. They felt that at Risinghill 'people really understood what autism was' and the staff were 'so calm – understanding and wanting him to succeed'. This family particularly enjoyed parent's evenings and liked the way in which they were 'talked to as parents...[which] enabled [them] to be part of a social network', in contrast to the previous secondary school that was 'very isolating'.

Another parent talked about how Risinghill staff 'were really tough with [their son] and didn't stand for his nonsense' but also did 'not blame him for getting angry and breaking things but tried to help him relax and manage his anger'. The parent recognised that this 'wasn't easy' but that it helped that the school 'took a real interest in the things he was interested in and didn't think he was weird. Teachers didn't call him names like the other school.'

What differences did you see over time?
One family commented that 'the family got to like him again instead of just shouting all the time.' They also noticed that their son had learnt 'that there were rules: how to behave, [including] private and public behaviour, so you can be daft with your friends, but sensible when grandparents are around.'

Another parent described her son's behaviour now: 'so much calmer, able to listen to adults. Now he is going to catering college and he knows he can say, "I don't understand – write it down."' This young adult 'still likes [and uses] his organiser' a year after leaving the school.

One other parent noticed that her son 'wanted to go to school; got up and got ready! He wanted to take things to show the teachers and he started having friends or people to phone.' This parent particularly appreciated that her son 'wasn't so angry at home' as frequently as he used to be.

Has your child used the strategies that they learnt at Risinghill since leaving?
Parents commented on the range of strategies that the young people learnt at Risinghill and continued to use in adult life. For instance, 'He uses his diary on his mobile phone, and always makes notes of things.' Also, 'His girlfriend loves it because he doesn't mind making shopping lists!'

Another young adult 'uses his breathing strategies all the time. He asks [his mother] for a massage or gives himself a hand massage on trigger points' for calming. His mother particularly appreciated that 'he knows how to apologise if something happens'.

What did you as parents learn?
One family remarked that they 'calmed down as a family; we stopped shouting and getting angry. We used to chant "write it down".' Another

realised 'that ASD is complex; that he wasn't just being a naughty boy. We tried to be firmer in making and keeping rules so that he didn't get so confused. We also have become more encouraging and praise him a lot more.' A mother described how empowering the strategy of written communication was for her: 'Instead of shouting at him I used to write it down on a list. You [the Headteacher] told me to walk away to calm down a bit.'

Other comments from families

The remarks from parents show how some students have made a typical transition into adult life. One student 'now lives with his girlfriend', his family 'see him every few weeks and he's coping. He can drive, goes on holiday abroad. He still has problems with money but he manages.' Other parents describe the value in the activities that they share with their child: 'He's different now: we talk more, enjoy each other's company and can go for long walks with the dogs.' One mother noted that 'I don't see him much now because he works away: he stays with friends or his uncle… He's like a grown up man – getting on.'

But were these changes things that would have occurred anyway, just through the passage of time and maturity?

This is the key question and the most difficult to answer given that this was not a research study. If we look at research, the overall conclusion of studies that have followed up people on the autistic spectrum from childhood into their adult lives is that things do get generally better over time – skills and understanding improve and some of the features of autism that are prominent in childhood decrease (Howlin 2009). However, this is research based on broad samples. It is not clear how applicable it is to the group of people we served at Risinghill. These are people with a long history of serious behavioural challenges, emotional difficulties and failure to access education. It is our experience as practitioners that the prospects for this group are often grim. They do not get better with time, their challenges and emotional difficulties increase and the sorts of outcomes that we have experienced are that these young people often end up in one or more of the following:

- Prison.

- Secure mental health facilities.

- Challenging behaviour units.

They do not get an education, they do not get jobs and they are prone to develop problems with drugs and alcohol. Those that remain at home often end up totally isolated, spending most of their lives in their rooms and tyrannising the family home. It would most certainly be our contention that the work at Risinghill transformed the prospects for our students and that without that work the outcomes for them would have been extremely negative. Although this is our belief there is some support for it from the research carried out by Professor Phil Reed that is summarised in Appendix 2, which suggests that the trajectory for Risinghill students was different to that for other young people on the autistic spectrum in other educational establishments. However, what is really needed is more research focused on this issue so that we can establish more definitively what works and what does not. What we would want to stress at this point is that even the most difficult young people with ASD, at a particularly difficult stage in their lives, can be helped effectively to change the course that they are on. We would argue for optimism and active intervention and not fall for either:

- assuming they will grow out of it…and leaving them be

- assuming they will never grow out of it…and focusing on 'managing' them.

We would argue for thoughtfulness, persistence and an appreciation of the extraordinary people that lie hidden from us by the magnitude and chronicity of their behavioural presentation. Without a 'go for it' mentality nothing will change. With that mentality and a large toolkit of practical supports transformation becomes a possibility.

Chapter 12

ORGANISATIONAL SUPPORTS

Throughout the book we have discussed the organisational supports that were involved in the practical work of Risinghill. We will use this chapter to summarise and expand on the topic, both to ensure fuller coverage and as a help to those who might want to move their own organisations in a new direction.

Background

The work of Risinghill had a number of important background characteristics. At its heart is a psychological approach rather than a technological approach. By this we mean that the work was based on an understanding of why certain things were happening, whether it was the behaviour of students or the behaviour of staff; and then designing what was to be done on the basis of this understanding. Interventions were therefore often generated or created anew. This contrasts with the more straightforward application of specific learnt technologies such as TEACCH or ABA for people with autism, where a well worked out set of procedures is applied to people just on the basis of an identifying label (autism) rather than on an understanding of their individual needs. This is not to criticise the technological approach – indeed many such technologies were used at Risinghill. However, we were trying to add to that way of doing things. The psychological base was broad but drawn from the mainstream empirical psychologies (developmental, social, behavioural, cognitive) rather than from more psychodynamic perspectives.

A second key aspect of the work was that we were attempting to develop a problem-solving community, a systemic or whole school approach rather than a series of plans for individual pupils. Of course individual plans were an important tool but they were part of a broader approach to helping all pupils and staff to develop.

Foreground

At the organisational level the work had a number of specific components. Some were related to what we were trying to achieve, others to how we were trying to achieve it.

A clear sense of purpose

The whole point of the work was to help both students and staff gain in skills, understanding, well-being and self-confidence so that they could move on successfully to claim lives that would work for them at the next stage. It was not just about hitting specific targets or bench-marks, but achieving things that would impact on the quality of life now and lead to transformation in longer term future prospects.

An empathic but challenging view of those involved

We sought always to understand why students and staff did what they did but with a view to moving things forward. We had high expectations for everyone and confidence that these expectations could be fulfilled.

An open system, a problem solving rather than an authoritarian style

We saw the whole system as a learning system so that change, evolution and innovation were expected. There were no set answers but through a process of collaborative problem solving things would be moved forward. This contrasts with more hierarchical and directive approaches such as 'management by objective', where senior management/staff push through top-down changes with very limited involvement from those who are the target of change. Objectives at Risinghill were important in so far as they helped us to be more efficient problem solvers but they were not an end in themselves.

Leadership

Although the approach emphasised involvement and open-mindedness, this was not a democracy or a commune. The role of the leader was absolutely critical. She brought the knowledge, the experience, the vision and the drive without which the work described in this book could not have occurred. She brought the stability so that a system evolved and developed despite the inevitable turnover of students and staff. Change needs to be led, a point to which we will return later in the chapter.

External consultants

This type of work benefits from the input of external consultants. They can provide a view of situations that is different from those dealing with those situations day in, day out. This can enrich the quality of problem solving. But they can and should also bring something more to the table, some kind of specific expertise that is needed for the work but is unlikely to be found in many of the staff charged with carrying out the work. What was brought to the school was the application of psychology, from both a clinical and educational psychologists' perspective. This was successful because the head as leader wanted to work with the educational and clinical psychologists. She had a strong belief in the value of applied psychology within a system. Her view was that the tasks were shared collaboratively in working and learning together in a creative way. The emphasis was upon the environment of the students, including our own behaviour, and how that might be involved in triggering responses by the students. Through understanding psychology the three authors came with a belief system that change is possible; and this view was communicated to all staff so that the focus was on what they could do rather than just focusing on the problems 'within the child'. Staff were aware of the issues that the individual students were bringing, but did not use these as a reason for not being able to change things.

A heavy investment in training

As the staff were charged with educating the students, so it seemed equally important to ensure proper educational input for the staff to enable them to do the best job possible. Training was influenced by known and successful approaches such as Portage and Training in EDY (Education of the Developmentally Young, see Chapter 10). It was devised and written initially by the authors in order to make it applicable to everyday life in the classroom at Risinghill. The Learning Environment for Autistic Development (LEAD) was a training approach that was available to all staff and was practised through role play and practice in the classrooms (see Chapter 10). Once this approach became embedded the experienced staff were then encouraged to share their expertise with others, thus creating a cascade of learning and an enhanced sense of ownership of the approaches involved.

Another approach for staff who were not in managerial roles was to support them through regular coaching. This involved staff working in small groups and bringing any work-related issues to their team of peers and the educational psychologist to help them think through and plan for solutions. The coaching went through systematic phases of information gathering, analysing, reflecting and action planning.

Attention to the quality of the physical and social environment

Although less discussed in this book it was regarded as very important that the physical environment was attractively decorated and kept in a good state of repair. Notices and signs were clear, relevant and uncluttered. Likewise messages about the social environment in the school were clear (for example, through the rule/mantra of 'say it straight' to encourage open communication about concerns) and positive (for example, through the use of 'treats' of one sort or another, from cakes to massages!). The head's belief in nurturing everyone, staff and visitors as well as students, was evident for all to see. This fits with Maslow's hierarchy of needs (Maslow 1943, 1970) in that higher level needs can only be addressed if people have their physical needs considered and feel comfortable and safe. As part of this overall effort time was built into the school year for staff to 'walk the building' to look and see if it was 'autism friendly'.

The adoption of specific techniques

Within our broadly psychological perspective we looked to both research and experienced practitioners to help us find solutions to the problems that we faced. These are detailed throughout the book. Most of the techniques were mainstream (for example, visual communication, use of consequences to influence behaviour), although they often progressed in highly innovative ways (see the ways in which visual supports were used). Others such as massage were more unusual at the time although have since become a more acceptable part of practice. Others again, such as mantras and the relationship style, were unique to the school.

The development of a 'house style'

It was seen as important to develop the notion of 'this is how we do things here' and to emphasise the distinctiveness of the work. Thus when people came to work for us they were signing up to more than the usual employment contract, they were signing up to do things in specific ways. This was expressed through day-to-day conversation, acronyms, the staff induction handbook, training…all building that idea of 'the Risinghill way'.

So, if you put together these organisational features, specific techniques and day-to-day implementation, you have what is described in this book and this was very different from what went on before. This was a process of organisational change that led to the outcomes that we have described. This raises the issue of how organisations can be changed, and what is involved in moving an organisation on so that it does things differently. We have described key features and outcomes achieved, but getting this process started is a challenge for any headteacher. In the last section we will reflect on some of the key things that help organisations to change.

Organisational change
Change requires leadership

Someone in line management authority within an organisation is needed to lead change. The leader should have relevant technical skills and some idea of where she wants to take the organisation but not a complete blueprint. The essence of this approach is to involve everyone in collaborative developments and to see learning as a key element, so that one has to be open to things moving in unanticipated directions. If the leader already has a clear blueprint and simply wants that executed then a much more hierarchical top-down approach is indicated, rather than the system we have described here.

Leaders need support

Leading change requires something more than a 'hero innovator' (Georgiades and Phillimore 1975), a lone individual battling to lead the move to a better future. A change leader needs support at a number of levels. It will be important to identify early on staff who are ready and willing to take on new ideas and who will support change efforts. Equally important is to look up the hierarchy, to identify one or more people at senior levels in the organisation (above the head) who support the need for change. Change is always resisted. This is a natural psychological response. There will be a lot of time spent trying to stop or undermine changes and this can come at all levels in an organisation, above and below. The leader is well positioned to deal with staff resistance, but will need support from more senior advocates (such as members of the governing body) to deal with the more senior saboteurs. It needs to be understood that leading an organisation through changes can be quite isolating and stressful. External consultants play an important role in supporting the leader at a personal level as well as the specific technical expertise that they bring to the work.

A long-term perspective

Changes in an organisation can sometimes be made quickly, but such changes rarely last. As a rough rule of thumb expect for it to take at least two years to initiate change, to train and then to embed significant changes within an organisation. The need to ensure that there is a shared construction by the staff of the school's new developments is crucial. Watkins (2004) writes about the role of teachers in 'leading learning' and this should be as much in the learning of the staff as the pupils. At Risinghill the leadership was certainly distributed as a part of the process of building the culture. This meant that the philosophy and beliefs were shared by the staff so that they could work together in their new endeavour. However, building this kind of momentum takes time.

Start with raising awareness

For change to make sense there has to be a vision that things can be different and improved, in this case a vision that children can come to school and learn in ways that harness their strengths. Thus there has to be a phase where the effort is directed at making sure that everyone is made aware that there is a problem with the status quo. You can be quite sure that many people in the organisation will be quite comfortable with the status quo and see no reason to change. There needs to be some 'unsettling' to prepare the way for what will follow. The challenge offered to staff was to overcome the problem that students with ASD reach adult life without the skills and approaches needed to hold down a job. The challenge in fact was how to help transform the students' approach to being in the local community so that they could achieve successful, long-term employment. This had to begin with changing the curriculum on offer to that of 'real world learning' so that the students gradually developed their skills and confidence while going through the apprentice phase, succeeded in work experience and then gained and maintained a place at work.

Get staff involved in focusing the 'mission'

As awareness of the need for change is raised then staff need to be drawn into the exercise of defining what change is supposed to achieve – what will be the outcomes that we are striving for. Clarity is needed about who we serve and what we hope to achieve for them that is different from what is going on now. Investment of time and energy is needed to develop a shared sense of purpose that is written into hearts and minds, not just on paper. The shared purpose was to find particular niches of interest and work in which each individual student could flourish. Thus an interest in lining up cars might lead on to being a mechanic in adult life, or an obsession with wildlife to becoming a game-keeper.

Put more effort into walking through open doors than kicking down closed ones

Since change will be resisted it is likely that the naysayers will dominate the leader's time and attention. Although it is important to try and get as many people as possible on board with change and time needs to be given to listening to concerns, it is even more important to identify those who are either keen or just willing to try new things. It is vital to nurture these people and build up the force for change through them. Thus care is needed to ensure that more attention is given to the positive forces than to the resistive forces.

Manage by walking about

This harks back to the management literature of the 1980s and 1990s (for example, Peters 1989) but remains a very key point to understand. You cannot bring about change by memos, meetings and appraisals. You need to be working alongside people, helping them to solve real life problems in real life situations. Thus those who are leading the change at the management level must make sure that they have time to observe and to work alongside the staff whose behaviour they want to change. At Risinghill the head and senior staff were in the classrooms, modelling approaches and offering support. Again, the focus is on the good things and encouragement for getting things right not endless criticisms for things that are wrong. A useful rule of thumb is that positive interactions should outweigh critical or corrective interactions at a ratio of 3:1.

Use training to support ongoing change not to initiate change

As we have emphasised, significant investment in training was seen as an essential component of the work at Risinghill. However, training is not in itself much good at initiating change. Heavy investment in training at the start of a programme of change, as a means of getting change going, is a widely used, massively expensive and a hugely ineffective approach. Rather, training needs to be used to support and to extend changes that are already under way. It also needs to be seen as something for everyone not just a remedial tool for junior staff. Thus on most occasions the head and/or senior staff at Risinghill were active participants in any new training, and were part of the learning taking place for the whole staff group. This meant that all staff could see that senior management were also practising new skills and approaches which in turn built up the confidence to show videos on work with individual students that was then discussed in a multi-professional group. This joint learning also keeps the link between training and the management process so that what is learnt in training is supported day-to-day by this process.

Develop the 'brand'

As change gets under way it is important to start defining and branding the 'house style', 'the way we do things here'. This will give people a sense of being special and different in a celebratory way (an important subtext when working with devalued groups). This can be expressed through acronyms for the work, bespoke assessment formats and other paperwork, particular phrases or key words that are used in day-to-day discussions, particular formats for celebrations and other organisational events. There are many examples throughout the book, but it is about looking for every way of communicating that 'this is us and we are special'.

Line up new staff induction with the change that is under way

Significant staff turnover is a fact of organisational life. If you are in a process of change it is vital to communicate with prospective new staff what the job in this organisation will be about and if they come into post, induct them into the ways that you want them to practice. It is fatal to neglect this area and to let them by default be inducted into the 'old ways'. At Risinghill the induction was led by skilled and experienced staff who could model specific approaches for new team members. New staff were encouraged to learn from a range of colleagues by identifying specific staff whose practice was exemplary in certain areas – for example, 'Go to Mark the chef to see how to give positive praise,' 'See how Jason's room is set up with clear, unambiguous displays,' 'Jane can demonstrate the use of mind-mapping on the flip-chart.'

Remember that there is no such thing as the 'promised land'

Sometimes we think about change as moving from one state to another (better) state and then stabilising. Indeed some organisations move in this kind of way. This results often in cycles that alternate reasonable practice with unacceptable practice. It seems that stopping often leads to drift and regression. This cycle is a terrible curse in services for devalued and disadvantaged people. The reasons for this are many and complex and a full discussion is beyond the scope of this book. However, understanding that this is the case means that a different view of change has to be adopted. This is the idea of continuous improvement, that there is a constant flow of information about how established practices and innovations are working out and that adjustments are constantly made in the light of the feedback received. This is a model of inherent instability. Thus the work described in this book is not a final report – it is not about how things need to be. It is an interim report on a work in progress, a work that is essentially never ending. It is about a journey not an arrival. Thus the change leader has to consider what to do once the initial goals are reached. Does one stop there and say, 'This is it and this is how we will carry on' or does one acknowledge that this is where we have got to and now we need to consider the next moves? This can involve the change leaders in difficult decisions. Leading change is exhausting work. Having led a major organisational change one may not have the energy to keep up the process of continuing improvement. One may need to look for some other kind of role. Or it may be that the lure of further change is exciting and one is up for the job. Either way it is a tough decision for the person/people who have played the key role(s) in leading an organisation through a major change. What is not an option is to say, 'This is where we are and this is where we will stay.' That way lays disaster.

So the chapter ends, the book is finished, but not the story.

REFERENCES

Clements, J. (1987) *Severe Learning Disability and Psychological Handicap*. Chichester: John Wiley and Sons.

Clements, J. (2005) *People with Autism Behaving Badly: Helping People with ASD Move On from Behavioural and Emotional Challenges*. London: Jessica Kingsley Publishers.

Clements, J. and Martin, N. (2002) *Assessing Behaviours Regarded as Problematic for People with Developmental Disabilities*. London: Jessica Kingsley Publishers.

Dessent, T. (1984) *What is Important about Portage?* Windsor: NFER.

Frohman, A.H., Weber, S.J. and Wollenburg, K. (1983) *The Portage Home Teaching Book*. Wisconsin: Cooperative Educational Service Agency.

Georgiades, N.J. and Phillimore, L. (1975) 'The myth of the hero innovator and alternative strategies for organizational change.' In C.C. Kiernan and E.P. Woodford (eds) *Behaviour Modification with the Severely Retarded*. Amsterdam: Associated Scientific Publishers.

Howlin, P. (2009) 'Outcome in adults with autistic spectrum disorders'. Paper presented at the Cambian Education Conference, May 2009.

Hughes, D. (2006) *Building the Bonds of Attachment: Awakening Love in Deeply Troubled Children*. Lanham, MD: Jason Aronson.

Leff, J.P. and Vaughn, C. (1985) *Expressed Emotion in Families: Its Significance for Mental Illness*. New York, NY: Guilford Press.

Maslow, A.H. (1943) 'A theory of human motivation.' *Psychological Review 50*, 4, 370–396.

Maslow, A.H. (1970) *Motivation and Personality*. Second edition. New York, NY: Harper and Row.

McBrien, J., Farrell, P. and Foxen, T. (1992) *Education of the Developmentally Young: Teaching People with Severe Learning Difficulties*. Second edition. Manchester: Manchester University Press.

Peters, T. (1989) *Thriving on Chaos*. London: Pan Books.

Rutter, M., Kreppner, J. and Sonuga-Barke, E. (2009) 'Emmanuel Miller Lecture: Attachment insecurity, disinhibited attachment, and attachment disorders: Where do research findings leave the concepts?' *Journal of Child Psychology and Psychiatry 50*, 5, 529–543.

Sears, W. and Sears, M. (2009) *The Attachment Parenting Book*. New York, NY: Little, Brown and Company.

Smull, M. and Allen, B. (1999) *Developing First Plans: A Guide to Developing Essential Lifestyle Plans*. Napa, CA: Allen, Shea and Associates.

Truax, C.B. and Carkhuff, R.R. (1967) *Towards Effective Counseling and Psychotherapy: Training and Practice*. Chicago, IL: Aldine.

Volkmar, F., Paul, R., Klin, A. and Cohen, D. (2005) *Handbook of Autism and Pervasive Developmental Disorders*. Third edition. New Jersey, NJ: John Wiley and Sons.

Watkins, C. (2004) *Learning and Leading*. Nottingham: National College for School Leadership.

Westmacott, E.V.S. and Cameron, R.J. (1981) *Behaviour Can Change*. London: Macmillan.

Appendix 1

SAMPLE STAFF TRAINING MATERIALS

Curriculum guidance to promote positive behaviour in everyday practice working with students

Note: Students will need all staff to be consistent in their approach.

1. I'm in charge

We need to remind students that our task is to teach.

Staff should always speak to students using their names, smiling and showing basic courtesy.

Principle	Practice		
	Resource	Action	Verbal
Greet students as they enter the class or gather for an activity.	Big Book.	Open hand posture ready for pointing and gesturing.	Welcome/ greeting.
Direct students where to sit or stand to start the session:		Put resources on table ready to touch.	'We're (what) in/on (where) for (why/what session)'.
If students are waiting we define the waiting activity.		Wide stance. Stand tall.	
Stand or sit, so that you can scan all the students. Direct students to move closer if they need additional support with focusing attention.		Open facial expression.	

2. Ready to learn

Students need an opportunity to transition into learning mode and to remind them of roles.

Principle	Practice		
	Resource	Action	Verbal
Students need to be calm to learn. Practice calm breathing:	Big Book – Body Basics Programme.	Demonstrate the gestures of listening, thinking and enquiry.	We're getting ready to learn.
Breathe and blow strategies.			Calm breathing gives me a good supply of oxygen for thinking.
Brain gym activity.		Hands on head.	
Students need to be sitting or standing in a looking and listening posture.		Hands on chest. Hands on stomach. Hands on knees/resting against stomach.	Hands in my lap to help me listen.
Adults need to model the learning postures:			At work adults take time to think.
a calm approach to the activity.		Feet on floor.	
Remember:		Hand on hip and hand on jaw.	
One Big Talker			
All other adults are shapers.			

3. Setting the scene

Principle	Practice		
	Resource	Action	Verbal
Students need to know: 1. What they are doing. 2. Where they are doing it. 3. When they're finished (time-based or productivity based). 4. Who will be there to help. 5. What their rewards will be. N.B. Tangible rewards can be given in addition to points. Students need to have the social reason/purpose/function for the task made explicit.	Big Book. Session plan. Task instructions. Staff roles. Personalised in organiser. Sticker chart. Weekly reward sheet in organiser.	Look and Point to key words in the Big Book. Looking at student organiser/task folders.	We have... tasks. Open your organiser: Check your tasks. Don't forget/ I'm reminding you/remember you are working to earn your points.

4. Ready Steady Go

Principle	Practice		
	Resource	Action	Verbal
Students are in charge of their learning.	Task instructions.	I know you can do this.	What's next?
Students need a visual structure and task instruction which they are in charge of (e.g. ticking off). Students need visual support to facilitate asking for help.	Task instructions/ structured support.	Use graphic supports to remind and shape behaviour.	What could you do now? Check your instructions.

5. It's not OK

Principle	Practice		
	Resource	**Action**	**Verbal**
Students need consistent feedback regarding on-task and off-task behaviour.	Class rules. Big Book. Student organiser.	Praise another member of the group for doing what you want them to do. Describe the behaviour.	I really like the way you are... You are ... Well done. I like... It's not OK to... I'm reminding you, your task is...
If the only person being affected by the behaviour of a student is the Big Talker, then that behaviour can be tactically ignored.			
The shaper should now move closer to the student and use graphic prompts as reminders.			We work in a considerate way... I'm reminding you, your task is...
Physical aggression is never OK.			
When students are reminded of their task (e.g. to sit at the table, give thinking and take-up time).			

6. Staying calm

Principle	Practice		
	Resource	**Action**	**Verbal**
We use repetition of mantras in order to stay calm.

Staff need to show they are remaining calm.

Students who are abusive or aggressive to staff or students need to leave the learning environment.

Once students have left the learning environment, other students need to be calmed. | Graphic pack.

Wall charts.

Graphic cards. | Repeat the mantra.

Breathe!!! Use body talk/moves.

Instruct student to leave.

The shaper follows guidance in the Student's Behaviour Support Plan.

Use a body talk/ moves strategy through very clear modelling and gesture. | It's not OK.

Stay quiet.

You are…

It's too hard to talk about how to make this right, now. We can work it out later. Go to a bench and calm down.

This has been hard… |

7. Breaking school rules

Principle	Practice		
	Resource	**Action**	**Verbal**
All students learn together.	Student 'I need help' cards.		What would help you…?
Any disruption to the learning or well-being of others must be addressed fairly.	Warnings. Go to calming bench.		I'm reminding you, your task is…
In order for students to learn they have to choose to listen to staff instructions and make decisions.	Leave class card.		This is your first warning.
			If you continue to disrupt our learning you will need to stay behind. This is your second warning.
			This is the third warning. As you won't follow the instruction, you will have to leave the class now and finish your task (at break time/ lunch time/at home…).

8. Sanctions

Students who have broken the school rules need to be removed from the learning environment immediately.

The student is sent to meeting room or function room to meet with the Duty Manager.

Both staff and student complete an incident sheet independently.

Students will have a fair hearing in order that an appropriate consequence is agreed.

The Duty Manager who gives the sanction must complete the incident sheet.

9. It's a wrap and well-done

Principle	Practice		
	Resource	**Action**	**Verbal**
At the end of a session students need to have the learning achievements made explicit. They must gain an insight into their progress. Students are helped to recognise their own achievement and receive rewards for these.	Flip-chart: Mind-map the positive achievements. Task instructions. Session plan. Sticker charts. Reward sheet in organiser and tangible rewards.	Use BERIS framework for thinking.	What did you do (B), what helped you (E) who helped you/who did you work with (R), what were you good at (I). What will you use again (S); what will you change next time (S)? Did you stay in the session? Did you complete your tasks? Did people say good things about your work?

10. What's next?

Principle	Practice		
	Resource	**Action**	**Verbal**
Students need the next task/session/location to be made explicit. Students need to be reminded how to move around site safely and appropriately.	Organiser, daily timetable. Graphic transition prompt. Rules in organiser.	Direct student to check their timetable. Staff to direct student to visual support.	'Check your timetable. Where are you going?' Remember we walk safely and quietly on the paths.

THE ROLE OF EDUCATIONAL PLACEMENT, EDUCATION PROVISION AND PARENTS ON THE SCHOOL PERFORMANCE OF CHILDREN WITH AUTISTIC SPECTRUM DISORDERS

Phil Reed,* Lisa A. Osborne and Emma Waddington
Swansea University

Abstract

A two-year investigation of the impacts of school placement and provision on the performance of pupils with autistic spectrum disorders (ASD) was conducted. A range of provisions, and extra-school factors, were examined to assess their effects on children with ASD. School placement (mainstream or special) was found to be largely irrelevant to the academic outcomes for children with ASD, although special placements had an advantage in terms of improving their social and emotional behaviours. In contrast, some aspects of school provision, and some parental factors, were found to be more important: speech and language therapy was found to improve academic performance, parenting stress levels and coping abilities played major roles in child outcomes. The performance of the children at Risinghill School was found to be at least as good, in terms of intellectual functioning, as children in other schools, and the social–emotional functioning of the children at Risinghill was improved relative to that seen in other schools (both special and mainstream); the reasons for this require exploration. The difficulties of conducting such research, and some methodological suggestions, are also presented.

Background and aims

This report is based on a two-year-long study that investigated the impacts of various forms of school placement and provision, and parental factors,

---

* Correspondence address: Phil Reed, Department of Psychology, Swansea University, Singleton Park, Swansea, SA2 8PP

on the performance of pupils with ASD at school. In particular, the study explored the impact of special versus mainstream school placements on both academic, and behavioural, outcomes for children with ASD. In addition to this focus, a range of educational provisions and 'extra-school' factors, irrespective of the actual school placement, were examined in order to assess which of these factors impacted on the children. In this respect, the role of the children's parents in determining outcomes was a key focus of this investigation, as the parents must be regarded as key partners with schools, and their influence not ignored in such studies.

Thus, it could be said that the current study adopted a 'systems' view, in which the development of the child with ASD at school is seen in a context involving not only school factors, but is also linked to the wider family situation. One view of the manner in which various factors impact upon the child with ASD can be seen in Figure Appx 2.1, which shows the interactions between child, parent and educational provisions, established through previous research work. Such a schematic representation is meant merely to guide thinking about these issues, rather than to suggest that a 'holistic' approach be favoured to the investigation of this area. The relationships between the variables may well be complex and dynamic in nature, but the only way forward in this area is through systematic research of these relationships.

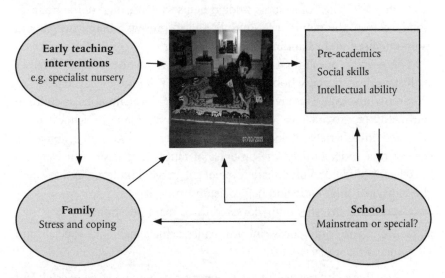

Figure Appx 2.1 Schematic representation of the interactions between child, school and parental factors

Research strategy

These issues were explored through a series of retrospective archival analyses, and prospective longitudinal studies, of the development of pupils with ASD who were attending a range of different provisions. Arising from these studies, a view of the impact of school placements (mainstream versus special), educational provisions and parenting effects, was developed across a range of measures concerning the pupils, including their intellectual, educational, and social–emotional and behavioural functioning.

The research strategy adopted had two components. The first was to try to develop an overall understanding of the effects of these general educational aspects on the school performance of children with ASD, in order to isolate generalisable findings across numerous school contexts. The second approach was embedded within the first, and gave a specific focus to the study of one particular educational establishment: in this case, to be known as Risinghill. Such a specific focus conducted in the context of a more general assessment of these issues, not only allowed an assessment of this particular centre, described in detail in this book, but also allowed greater understanding of the effects of specific forms of provision (highlighted from the more general study) to be examined in a way that can not be obtained from a more overarching study. In turn, the information obtained about the effects of placements and provisions from the wide range of schools studied helps to contextualise the findings obtained from the pupils at Risinghill, and to present a better overall and contextualised understanding of their progress.

The specific questions tackled in this report revolve around whether mainstream or special school placement is best suited to meet the needs of children with ASD. The investigation involved a large number of children with ASD (approximately 300), placed in a wide range of schools (over 50), and in a variety of local authorities (over 15). As noted above, as part of this wider project, the progress of children at Risinghill was also specifically studied to illuminate some of the general findings, and to show the impact of this centre and its provisions in itself.

Overall, the investigation addressed three main questions:

1. Are there differences in academic achievement in special and mainstream placements?

2. Are there differences in socio-emotional outcomes in special and mainstream placements?

3. How well do children in Risinghill progress compared with children in other placements?

School inclusion

Current legislation encourages the inclusion into mainstream schools of all children with special educational needs, including children with ASD, whenever this is possible. In this context, the term 'inclusion' is used, in a wide sense, to describe the movement of children into mainstream schools, who would otherwise have been educated in special schools. This movement is premised on the 'rights' of a child to education, initially promoted in the UK by Warnock (1978), among others, and this basis for inclusion has been encouraged by various agencies and governments; for example, by UNESCO, through the Salamanca Statement (1994), and this statement forms an important basis for current policy (DES 1981; IDEA 1997).

However, it should be noted that, while the implementation of such a policy may lead to an 'inclusive' education in that all children are educated together, it is not clear that this is an education that actually meets the needs of all children with special educational needs (Lindsay 2003; Ofsted 2006). Indeed, this fact has been acknowledged by the initial architect of the 'inclusion policy' (Warnock 2005). Although there may be an ongoing, and heated, philosophical debate about the concept of 'inclusive' education, it has to be noted that there is a paucity of empirical evidence regarding whether or not such an inclusive policy promotes the most effective education for children with ASD.

Although relatively few in number, there are some studies that have observed the effects of inclusion in mainstream schools for children with ASD, but these studies have reported mixed results. In terms of the educational or academic performance of children with ASD in various school placements, one of the few studies that assessed the development of children with ASD was conducted by Harris et al. (1990). This report assessed increases in the ratio between developmental level and rate of language use, by employing the Preschool Language Scale, in segregated versus integrated provision. Harris et al. (1990) found no significant differences between the developmental level, and the rate changes, between students with ASD in the two settings, suggesting no difference in mainstream and special school in terms of the academic/educational advances of the children in those placements.

It has been argued that social behaviour, rather than academic outcomes, may be the domain with the greatest potential to benefit from inclusive settings (see Harris and Handleman 1997). This aspect of children's development has received slightly more study than academic outcomes, but there still remains a relative lack of information about this issue. Strain

(1983) focused on preschool, and primary, school children with ASD, and found that children in mainstream schools exhibited more pro-social behaviours than their special school peers. Similarly, Buysse and Bailey (1993) documented greater improvements in social skills (defined as social behaviour and play skills) in inclusive settings compared to segregated school settings. However, in contrast to these positive results, several other studies have shown no such pattern of gains for children educated in mainstream placements (Durbach and Pence 1991; Harris *et al.* 1990). Thus, the impact of the school placement on the social behaviour of children with ASD remains unclear.

Even based on the above very brief summary of the literature, it can be seen that the research on the benefits of including a child with ASD in mainstream is far from conclusive. The lack of substantial evidence indicating the benefits of mainstream school placement that was anticipated by the proponents of inclusion, have allowed critics of the inclusion agenda to argue that the movement of children into mainstream schools has been primarily driven by ideological arguments. Irrespective of the impact of this lack of evidence for wider educational policy, such a lack of conclusive evidence, coupled with a drive towards mainstreaming children with ASD, obviously has implications for special schools, including Risinghill. Critically, this issue impacts directly on many children and their families (as it does for each and every special school), and clearly deserves much further empirical investigation than it has currently received.

In the light of these considerations, the current study aimed to compare the progress of children with ASD placed in mainstream schools with the progress of children with ASD placed in special schools, and, as part of this project, the progress of children in Risinghill. Although these questions are, admittedly, somewhat blunt (see Ryan 2009; Warnock 2005), they are questions that have had produced large amounts of debate, but which has had surprisingly few empirical analyses. This report is among the first to address these issues empirically, and its findings, especially when read in conjunction with the description of Risinghill given in this current volume, are hoped to throw some light on this critical educational issue, and on the likely effectiveness of the Risinghill type of education for children with ASD.

School placement
Academic progress
To address the impact of school placement on the academic performance of children with ASD, the records of 108 children with ASD (aged 5–16

years; mean = 13 years old), placed exclusively in one form of educational placement (e.g. special school or mainstream school) were studied. A range of measures in these educational archives were accessed to allow assessment of the effects of the children's autistic severity, their school placement, and the sorts of provision that they received over their school career, on the pupils' academic performance. Particular focus was given to the pupils' 'real world' academic achievement, based on their national curriculum results, rather than on their intellectual functioning, measured by standardised test IQ. While the latter psychometric assessment would produce reliable and standard measures, the former national curriculum results may have a greater level of external or ecological validity.

The degree to which the children's autistic diagnostic category, and their autistic severity, predicted their school placements, and the types of provision that the pupils received, were studied. The data that were extracted from the archives relating to these issues are displayed in Table Appx 2.1 and 2.2.

Table Appx 2.1 shows the autistic severity and symptoms of the pupils in four different types of educational placement (mainstream schools, special schools, special units in mainstream schools, and home education). These data reveal that the majority of pupils were exclusively placed in mainstream education, but that there were very few differences in the severity of the children's autism (as measured by the Autism Behaviour Checklist, ABC) across these different educational placements.

Table Appx 2.1 Severity of ASD as measured by the Autism Behaviour Checklist (ABC) in the different placements

| | | School placement | | | |
		Mainstream	Special	Unit	Home
ASD severity (Mean scores)	Total ABC (31–155)	80	74	77	78
	Sensory subscale (0–27)	11.5	9.5	11	11
	Relating subscale (4–38)	22.5	19	22	22

continued

Table Appx 2.1 Severity of ASD as measured by the Autism Behaviour Checklist (ABC) in the different placements *cont.*

	School placement			
	Mainstream	Special	Unit	Home
Body and object use subscale (0–31)	14	13.5	13	14
Language subscale (0–31)	12.5	15	14	14.5
Social and self help skills subscale (6–25)	16	17	17	17

Table Appx 2.2 displays the pupils' autistic diagnostic category, and the percentage of the children receiving various types of provision, depending upon the pupils' school placement. Similarly to the previous data, there were no great differences in the types of provision that the children received in those placements.

Together, these analyses suggests that school placement and provision is not systematically associated with the nature and severity of children's ASD, at least across the local authorities being studied in this report. Given that there were a large number of authorities involved in this study, there is no reason to assume that this finding would not be replicated elsewhere.

As there were no differences in the autism severity, diagnosis, or provision, between the pupils exclusively educated in mainstream schools and those educated either exclusively in special schools or in special units, these two groups of pupils were compared with one another. Given the lack of differences in the pupils' autism or provision, these data allow comparison between the placements in terms of their impact on academic outcome. That is, apart from the placement in mainstream or special school, there were few differences between the pupils, or their treatment, in these placements.

Table Appx 2.2 Differences in ASD severity and provision by school placement

		School placement (number in brackets)			
		Mainstream	Special	Unit	Home
Diagnosis	ASD	65% (51)	20% (16)	14% (11)	0% (0)
	AS	77% (14)	17% (3)	5% (1)	0% (0)
	ASD/co-morbid	50% (6)	33% (4)	0% (0)	11% (2)
SLT	Yes	78% (32)	88% (14)	88% (7)	No data
	No	22% (9)	12% (2)	12% (1)	No data
LSA	Mean hours (1–35)	18	19	19	19
	Percent-age receiving	100%	100%	100%	100%
Portage	Yes	8% (6)	8% (2)	33% (4)	0% (0)
	No	92% (65)	91% (21)	66% (8)	100% (2)
Social skills training	Yes	27% (19)	35% (8)	42% (5)	0% (0)
	No	73% (52)	65% (15)	58% (7)	100% (2)

In order for the impact of the school provision on the children's academic performance to be investigated, the data on national curriculum results of the children were assessed. These data were used to give a focus on 'real world' academic performance. To create an index that can be analysed, a P-level 1 in national curriculum was scored as 1, P-level 2 was scored as 2, P-level 3 as 3, and so on, up to P-level 8 as 8, and then, Level 1 was scored as 9, Level 2 as 10, and so on.

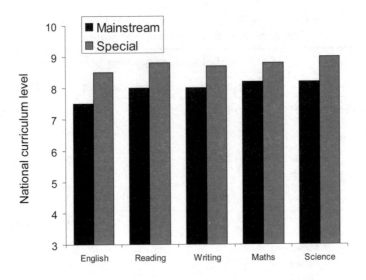

Figure Appx 2.2 Effect of school placement on academic outcomes

Figure Appx 2.2 shows this impact of the two types of placement (mainstream versus special and unit) on the national curriculum performance of the children. Inspection of Figure Appx 2.2 reveals that the overall level of performance of the pupils was around P-level 8, which is, of course, much lower than would be expected for a cohort of this mean age (13 years old). Further inspection shows that there was a very slight advantage for pupils in the special placements over the mainstream schools in terms of national curriculum results. However, these differences were not great in magnitude, and suggest no great impact on the academic achievement of the children.

Social and emotional outcomes

To study this aspect of children's functioning, children with ASD were followed over approximately one full school year in each setting (either exclusively in mainstream or exclusively in special education). This design was adopted to allow the initial level of ability of the children to be assessed, and the re-assessment at follow-up could identify any improvements due to the placement. The focus of this study was on standardised measures of social and adaptive behaviours, as it is often argued that the main benefit of including children with ASD is the potential for social gains through modelling from their normal developing peers (see Boutot and Bryant 2005).

Twenty mainstream schools took part in this part of the study, and there were 39 special schools in the study. The mainstream schools were generally of a similar size to one another (smallest = 212; largest = 498; mean = 321; SD = 106), and had a comparable number of students with statements of special educational needs attending their school (mean percentage = 2.3; SD = 1.2). The special schools in the study were smaller in size than the mainstream schools (size range 22 to 99; mean = 74; SD = 45.5).

A total of 83 children with an ASD diagnosis (aged 5–16) were included in this study. Each pupil had a baseline assessment, and then a follow-up assessment 9 to 10 months later (i.e. one school year). The children were measured in terms of a range of different aspects of their functioning, but, in particular, the focus of this part of the study was on their autistic severity (using the Autism Behaviour Checklist, ABC), and their social and emotional functioning (measured using the Strengths and Difficulties Questionnaire, SDQ).

Table Appx 2.3 Groups of children included in the longitudinal study

Sample	N	Variables	Mean	SD
Mainstream group	27	Age	8.0	2.9
		Autistic severity	80.7	16.1
High severity special group	35	Age	8.9	2.6
		Autistic severity	99.0	12.6
Low severity special group	21	Age	8.1	1.6
		Autistic severity	76.6	8.4

The children were broken down into three groups: one group of pupils placed in mainstream schools, and two groups of children who were placed in special schools. As the pupils in the special schools had a very wide range of severities of autism, these children were split into a high autistic severity group, and a low autistic severity group, such that there was no difference between the levels of autistic severity between the children in the low severity special school and the mainstream children. These data can be seen in Table Appx 2.3.

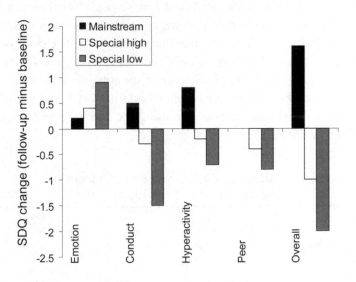

Figure Appx 2.3 Changes in the behavioural and emotional problems of children in the various school placements over a period of 9–10 months (low scores represent reductions in problems)

The change in the pupil's emotional and behavioural problem scores (as measured by the four subscales of the SDQ) from baseline to follow-up were then calculated (follow-up score minus the baseline score). These change scores for each problem scale are shown in Figure Appx 2.3. Decreases in these scores represent an improvement (a lessening) in the pupil's behaviour problems in the various domains measured. Inspection of these data shown in Figure Appx 2.3 reveals that, overall, the number of behavioural and emotional problems in a special school tended to decrease to a greater extent than those placed in a mainstream school. The important comparison to bear in mind when examining these data is that between the mainstream pupils and the special school pupils with lower autistic severity, as these two groups were best matched. This comparison clearly shows an advantage for children in the special school in terms of the behavioural and emotional development.

Mainstream versus special placement: summary

There was little evidence of systematic placement of children with ASD in various educational situations based on their characteristics. Most children had been placed in mainstream schools in line with governmental objectives. There was no evidence of superiority in terms of 'real world' academic performance of either special or mainstream schools, which replicates previous findings (Harris *et al.* 1990), and runs counter to the initial suggestions that prompted the inclusive movement (Warnock 1978). However, these data did suggest that special schools appear to offer an advantage in terms of the social and emotional improvements of the children (mainly for those with lower severity autism). This finding is one of the first to suggest that special schools do impart such an advantage. Thus, in summary, school placement *per se* was not a particularly strong predictor of academic outcomes, although children with ASD may fare better socially and emotionally in a special school.

Predictors of school performance

It might be suggested, notwithstanding the above results concerning social and emotional aspects of the pupil's functioning, that it is the provisions experienced with a school, rather than school placement *per se*, that is more important in predicting success (Warnock 2005). Thus, an important dimension of understanding the performance of pupils with ASD in school could be to explore the types of provision and support that they receive, irrespective of the nature of their school placement (i.e. mainstream or special). To this end, a finer-grained analysis of the data obtained from the preceding two studies (archive and longitudinal) allowed factors such as the child's autistic severity, and the nature of the provisions experienced in, or before, their school placement, to be examined with respect to their potential impact on children's performance.

Autistic severity

Based on the educational archive material held on the 108 children that were studied above, the relationship between the pupil's autistic severity (as measured by the ABC) and their national curriculum results was assessed (irrespective of school placement). These data showed that the severity of the pupil's autism was negatively correlated with their academic success (see Table Appx 2.4; the shaded areas of the table show the important significant results). Thus, the more severe the level of the pupil's autism, the worse were their national curriculum results. Although not surprising, this finding is important to note, as schools taking children with very severe autism should not necessarily be judged on this measure alone, relative to other schools.

Table Appx 2.4 Relationship between the children's ASD severity and their national curriculum performance

Outcome Subscale ABC	School placement	NC reading age	NC reading age comprehension	NC spelling	NC English	NC reading	NC writing	NC maths	NC science
Diagnosis	R=0.0 NS	R=0.1 NS	R=0.2 NS	R=0.0 NS	R=0.0 NS	R=0.2 NS	R=0.0 NS	R=0.0 NS	R=0.0 NS
Total score	R=0.1 NS	R=0.2 NS	R=0.2 $P<0.05$	R=0.0 NS	R=-0.3 $P<0.05$	R=-0.4 $P<0.001$	R=-0.4 $P<0.00$	R=-0.3 $P<0.05$	R=-0.3 $P<0.05$
Sensory	R=0.1 NS	R=0.1 NS	R=0.2 NS	R=0.0 NS	R=0.1 NS	R=-0.3 $P<0.05$	R=-0.3 $P<0.05$	R=-0.2 $P<0.05$	R=-0.3 $P<0.05$
Relating	R=0.1 NS	R=0.1 NS	R=0.2 NS	R=0.0 NS	R=-0.3 $P<0.05$	R=-0.3 $P<0.05$	R=-0.3 $P<0.05$	R=-0.3 $P<0.05$	R=-0.3 $P<0.05$
Body and object use	R=0.0 NS	R=0.2 NS	R=0.2 $P<0.05$	R=0.1 NS	R=-0.3 $P<0.05$	R=-0.4 $P<0.00$	R=-0.4 $P<0.00$	R=0.3 $P<0.05$	R=-0.3 $P<0.05$
Language	R=0.1 NS	R=0.2 NS	R=0.3 $P<0.05$	R=0.0 NS	R=-0.3 $P<0.05$	R=-0.3 $P<0.05$	R=-0.2 $P<0.05$	R=0.2 NS	R=0.1 NS
Social and self-help skills	R=0.0 NS	R=0.1 NS	R=0.2 $P<0.05$	R=0.1 NS	R=0.2 NS	R=-0.2 $P<0.05$	R=-0.3 $P<0.05$	R=-0.2 $P<0.05$	R=-0.2 $P<0.05$

School provisions

The types of provision that the pupils had received (e.g. social skills training, Portage, speech and language therapy, etc.) during or before their placements in school were also assessed through the archive study. Of course, such measures only indicate the presence and absence of various provisions, and not their quality or intensity. However, in the absence of other forms of data relating to this issue, these analyses represent a start in this neglected research area. The archive records noted that there was actually little relationship between having received many forms of provision and academic outcomes (e.g. social skills training, Portage) and the pupils' academic performance in terms of their national curriculum results.

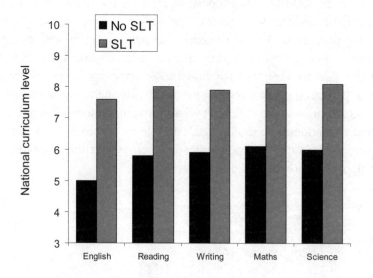

Figure Appx 2.4 Relationship between having had access to speech and language therapy and national curriculum results

However, having received speech and language therapy did appear to improve the academic performance of children with ASD, with those children who had received speech and language therapy performing better than those who did not have access to this provision across a range of academic measures (see Figure Appx 2.4). This finding is, of course, limited by the nature of the sample, and it may not be replicated in other contexts (see Osborne and Reed 2008a). Nevertheless, the findings of some positive relationships in some contexts, suggests that the impacts of such provisions require much greater and more detailed study.

Parental influences

Although children with ASD receive help and support at school, they spend the majority of their day with their parents and other care-givers. Ignoring the role of parents would be to miss both a significant factor that impacts on the children, and an opportunity to help the children. Thus, the current report assessed the degree to which parental influences impacted on the children's functioning.

Parenting stress

In research related to that reported here, 65 children (between 2.6 and 4 years old), and their parents, were studied over a nine-month period (see Osborne *et al.* 2008 for a full report) to examine the impact of parenting stress on the children's outcomes. The children were in various early education provisions, that were classified as being less time intense (up to 16 hours a week), and more time intense (over 16 hours a week). The children's parents were divided into those reporting lower and higher levels of parenting stress according to the Questionnaire on Resources and Stress (QRS) prior to the children's educational placement. Changes in the children's functioning in intellectual, educational and social domains over the period were noted (follow-up measures minus baseline measures), and these alterations are displayed in Figure Appx 2.5.

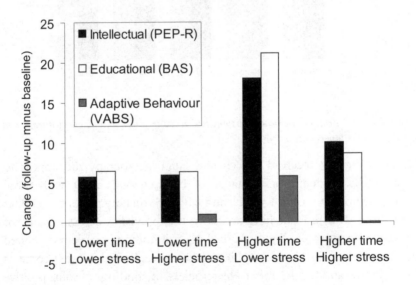

Figure Appx 2.5 Impact of teaching time intensity and parental stress on child gains over the period of nine months

Inspection of these data, shown in Figure Appx 2.5, reveals that higher time-intense interventions produced better gains for the pupils in terms of their educational functioning (measured by the British Abilities Scale (BAS)), and in terms of their social functioning (measured by the Vineland Adaptive Behaviour Scale), but higher levels of parenting stress levels reduced these improvements.

A very similar result was obtained in another study involving school-aged children in terms of the impact of parenting stress on the children's behaviour problems. Eighty-three children (aged 5 to 16 years old), and their parents, were studied over a nine month period (see Osborne and Reed 2009, for a full report). The children were in various school placements (mainstream and special), their parents were divided into lower and higher stress groups before the assessment period commenced, and the children's behavioural problems and improvements were noted. When there was higher parenting stress (as measured by either the Questionnaire on Resources and Stress, QRS, or by the Parenting Stress Index, PSI), there were worse child behaviour problems measured by the Strengths and Difficulties Questionnaire at follow-up (see Figure Appx 2.6).

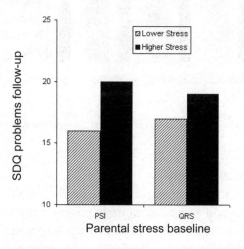

Figure Appx 2.6 Impact of parental stress on child behaviour problems in school-aged children over a period of nine months

Parental coping

Successful parental coping strategies are also implicated in the children's academic outcomes. Figure Appx 2.7 shows the national curriculum results for the children in the archive study as predicted by the types of coping strategy adopted by their parents (as measured by the F-COPES questionnaire). For children with lower severity autism, the adoption of 'reframing' coping strategies by the parent (i.e. attempting to change their perception of the 'problems'), works best for the child in terms of their academic outcomes. For children with higher severity, the parents' adoption of coping strategies that 'appraise' (accepting) the child's autistic severity, and the resultant constraints that this imposes on the child and themselves, actually works better for the child in terms of their academic performance.

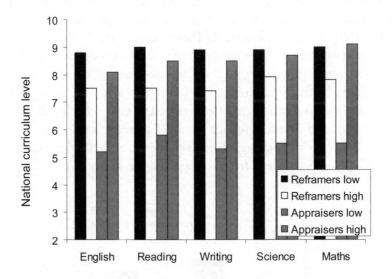

Figure Appx 2.7 The effect of different parental coping strategies on child academic outcomes

Parental influences: summary

In summary, parents are a major influence on their child, and a focus on school placement and provision alone is misguided. Parents of children with ASD have extremely high levels of parenting stress, which impacts negatively on their children's behaviours. A major issue after identifying these parent–child relationships is to discover why parenting stress impacts on the effectiveness of school placements and provision, and on the children's behaviour, as discovering this might aid to help parents and children. These relationships and their consequences have been discussed in some detail by Osborne (2009). Reducing these adversely high levels of parenting stress will help the child, and this may be achieved through helping the parent with behaviour management strategies, and to develop more productive coping styles. However, for the present purposes, it is clear that there are multiple influences between parents and professionals (including schools) that affect such variables. However, to be maximally effective any school, mainstream or special, needs to develop strong and positive relationships with the parents. Part of the assessment of any school, such as Risinghill, needs to focus on this aspect of their working practices.

The Risinghill School

As part of the investigation reported here, the impact of an educational placement at Risinghill was studied. This focus allowed this particular special school to be assessed, but also allowed the effects of the particular form of education given in the special school to be studied in more detail. So far, the general effects of mainstream and special schools have been studied, which is needed for the development of an overview of the situation, but specific focus allows specific provisions to be assessed in more detail. Notwithstanding the problems of external validity (generalisability), this can give some further insight regarding educational provision to be obtained. The chapters in this text have outlined in detail the provisions given in Risinghill, and this description, in conjunction with the general and specific results reported here, may shed further light on these educational issues for children with ASD. In addition to showing the impact of Risinghill on the pupils' performance, in itself, comparison of these data with those data outlined above, allows a contextualisation of these results, and better appreciation of this specific special school's impact on its pupils.

To this end, the performance of 12 children at Risinghill was assessed over a period of a full school year (i.e. nine to ten months). These children were aged between 11 and 14 years old, and they had moderately severe autistic symptoms according to the Autism Behaviour Checklist. The pupils were chosen for participation in this study as they were just starting their time at Risinghill. Thus, the study attempted to asses the impact of the first full year's placement at Risinghill on the pupils. These pupils were measured both in terms of their intellectual and educational functioning (using different aspects of the BAS), and in terms of their social and emotional functioning (using the Strengths and Difficulties Questionnaire).

Intellectual functioning

In order to assess the impact of placement at Risinghill on the intellectual functioning of its pupils, 12 children attending Risinghill were measured at baseline (at the start of their school year, and time at Risinghill), and again nine to ten months later at follow-up (at the end of their first school year at Risinghill).

These pupils were measured on five core performance scales of the British Abilities Scale (BAS: Designs, Word definitions, Patterns, Matrices and Verbal similarities). These scales produce a standardised score that reflects how well the pupil is doing relative to the general population of pupils of the same age. A score of 50 on these measures implies that the pupil is performing at the average level expected for a pupil of that age (across the whole population). A score lower than 50 implies that the intellectual functioning of the pupil is lower than the age-related mean performance; and a score on this measure of above 50, implies that the pupil is performing in advance of the average level for their age.

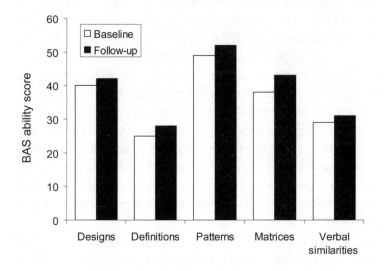

Figure Appx 2.8 The baseline and follow-up scores of Risinghill children on the subscales of the BAS

The data pertaining to the intellectual functioning of the pupils at Risinghill are shown in Figure Appx 2.8. Inspection of the baseline data taken at the start of the school year reveals that the performance of the children at Risinghill, as measured by the BAS standardised scores, ranged between 25 and 50. These scores indicate that the intellectual ability of these pupils was low relative to that which would be expected in the general population as a whole. When the pupils were measured again at the end of the school year, nine months later, these pupils showed largely unaltered standard scores relative to their baseline levels.

This pattern of results indicates that the pupils at Risinghill were maintaining their levels of ability relative to the general population. That is, the Risinghill pupils did not fall any further behind their peers over this period of time. Thus, although these standardised scores did not imply that there were any absolute improvements in the children's intellectual ability, they do imply that the skills of the pupils at Risinghill, as measured by the BAS scales, were progressing at the same rate as would be expected in the general population; that is, they were progressing at a rate commensurable with the development of a typically developing child, which, for children with ASD, who were actually quite intellectually impaired, is a strong result.

Educational functioning

The 12 children at Risinghill were also measured in terms of their educational functioning, according to the BAS achievement scales (Number skills, Spelling and Reading). Inspection of Figure Appx 2.9 shows that, at the baseline measure, the children's standard scores on all of these educationally-related abilities ranged between 60 and 80 (relative to a population mean of 100). These data suggest that, at the start of the school year, the pupils at Risinghill were performing at an educational level that was much lower than that normally seen in the general population.

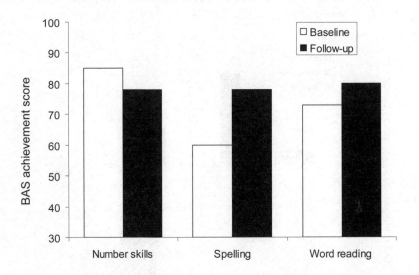

Figure Appx 2.9 The baseline and follow-up scores of Risinghill children in terms of their educational achievement scores (BAS)

By the end of the school year, the literacy skills of the children (i.e. their spelling and reading abilities) had increased by between 10 and 20 standard score. Such a result indicates that there had been an increase in the educational ability of the pupils at Risinghill relating to literacy, even relative to their actual age. That is, not only were the pupils maintaining their position relative to their typically developing peers, they were actually catching up with these peers over the nine to ten months of the school year that they were at Risinghill (although, it should be noted that they were still below the average in terms of educational levels). There was no improvement in their standard scores for the pupils' number skills, relative to their age.

Social–emotional functioning

Finally, the 12 Risinghill children were measured at the start of the school year (baseline), and again at the end of the school year (follow-up), on the four problem behaviour scales of the Strengths and Difficulties Questionnaire (SDQ: Emotional problems, Behaviour problems, Hyperactivity and Peer problems). The changes seen in these scores over time (follow-up minus baseline) for these pupils are shown in Figure Appx 2.10, as is the average change in emotional problems seen in pupils from the other mainstream and other special schools involved in this study. In terms of this change score, decreases over time reflect an improvement in the problem (i.e. it is getting less intense).

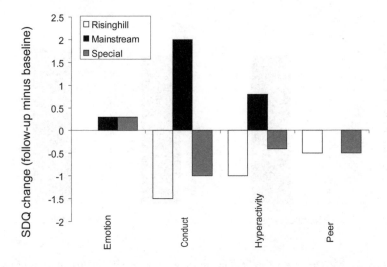

Figure Appx 2.10 The change (follow-up minus baseline) for the Risinghill children in terms of their behavioural problems (SDQ) relative to children in other mainstream and special schools

As can be seen from inspection of Figure Appx 2.10, the pupils at Risinghill demonstrated a reduction in their social and emotional problems which were at least as strong as the children in the other special schools involved in the larger-scale study, and the Risinghill pupils actually showed a greater decrease in these social and emotional problems than the pupils in the mainstream schools.

Summary of Risinghill influence

The results from the specific study of pupils at Risinghill should be assessed in the light of the description of the particular provisions experienced by these pupils (given elsewhere), as well as in the light of the overall findings reported for special and mainstream schools (above). The results reflect the impact of the first year at Risinghill on the pupils' performance, and they are limited to this extent. Nevertheless, they do allow further understanding of some specific provisions on pupils' performance, as well as allowing a validation of the type of educational approach on offer.

The pupils attending Risinghill demonstrated an increase in their intellectual performance in line with the advance in the pupils' actual chronological age, which is a significant achievement for children with ASD. There were also signs that the educational abilities of the children, in terms of their literacy, were accelerating over the period of the study while they were attending Risinghill. These specific intellectual and educational results are in line with the more general findings derived from the overall study. That is, children in special schools perform reasonably well compared to mainstream schools, and the performance of the children studied at Risinghill were no exception to this general rule (a finding that is impressive given their low levels of initial ability).

The Risinghill children's social and emotional behaviours also improved, and were, at least, as good as that typically seen in other special schools, and better than that seen in pupils with ASD attending mainstream schools. One feature of these data worth noting, is that the pupils' emotional problems are not worsening at Risinghill as the pupils get older, which often happens with pupils with ASD, and which contrasts to that seen in the pupils at mainstream schools studied here, and in other reports (see Osborne and Reed 2008b).

Overall, these findings suggest that pupils at Risinghill, given the specific educational provision that they receive, show as good progress as children in other special school contexts, and their particular improvements in social and emotional functioning is of interest for further study. Of course, the specific relationship of provision and outcome could be broken down even further in future studies, but the current findings are very promising for the Risinghill approach described here, and offer potential general insights of educational provision beyond this particular placement.

Summary

In relation to the issues of school placement and provision, this investigation came to a number of conclusions. In particular, it was noted that school placement issues, such as whether a pupil attended a mainstream or a special school, were found to be somewhat irrelevant to determining child progress. There were no differences in the academic outcomes for children with ASD between special and mainstream placements. On this basis, coupled with previous findings, there seems no reason to dismiss special education, either in the general, or in the specific, as being academically inferior, at least for pupils with ASD. As this was a major plank of the argument for inclusive education (Warnock 1978), it may well be time to review this policy more thoroughly. In contrast to a lack of difference in terms of academic achievement, special school placements in general were seen to have a slight advantage in terms of the pupils' social and emotional behaviours.

However, it should be noted that, overall, the type of educational provision and support, as well as parental factors, were found to be more important than school placement in predicting outcomes. In particular, speech and language therapy was found to improve academic performance irrespective of school placement. Parenting stress levels, and parental coping abilities, played major roles in child outcomes.

The particular performance of the pupils educated at Risinghill was at least as good in terms of intellectual functioning as children in other schools, but the social–emotional functioning of the children at Risinghill was in excess of that of some other schools, and the reasons for this require exploration. Perhaps investigation of educational provision is a type of study that can only be conducted by reference to the impacts of particular schools, such as Risinghill, where the exact nature of the day-to-day provision is better understood, and can be better related to pupil outcomes. The internal reliability of such studies is certainly higher than for more general studies, where the precise nature of the provision cannot be known with any degree of certainty. Such results may allow much to be learnt about what works for children with ASD in school. The downside of such specific studies is, of course, the constraints on the generality of the findings that may be inherent in them.

Thus, in addition to the particular results that emerged from this investigation, and their implications for the assessment of the Risinghill approach, a conclusion from such research is that such assessment may need to adopt this type of empirical grounded theory approach, where general initial findings are used to determine the sample that is specifically studied to isolate the effects of various provisions. The typical loss of generality that results from such specific studies may then be offset by back reference to the initial more general but less detailed studies. One investigation cannot determine these matters, but it is quite clear that further detailed empirical investigation is needed in this domain of education.

REFERENCES FOR APPENDIX 2

Boutot, A.E. and Bryant, D.P. (2005) 'Social integration of students with autism in inclusive settings.' *Education and Training in Developmental Disabilities 40*, 14–23.

Buysse, V. and Bailey, D.B. (1993) 'Behavioural and developmental outcomes in young children with disabilities in integrated and segregated settings: A review of comparative studies.' *Journal of Special Education 26*, 434–461.

Department for Education and Science (DES) (1981) *Education Act.* London: Her Majesty's Stationery Office.

Durbach, M. and Pence, A.R. (1991) 'A comparison of language production skills of preschoolers with special needs in segregated and integrated settings.' *Early Child Development and Care 68*, 49–69.

Harris, S.L. and Handleman, J.S. (1997) 'Helping children with autism enter the mainstream.' In D. Cohen and F.R. Volkmar (eds) *Handbook of Autism and Pervasive Developmental Disorders.* Second edition, pp.665–675. New York: Wiley.

Harris, S.L., Handleman, J.S., Kristoff, B., Bass, L. and Gordon, R. (1990) 'Changes in language development among autistic and peer children in segregated and integrated preschool setting.' *Journal of Autism and Developmental Disorders 20*, 23–31.

Individuals with Disabilities Education Act (IDEA) (1997) 20 US Congress: Chapter 33, Sections 1400–1491.

Lindsay, G. (2003) 'Inclusive education a critical perspective.' *British Journal of Special Education 30*, 3–12.

Office for Standards in Education (Ofsted) (2006) *Inclusion: Does it Matter where Pupils are Taught?* London: Ofsted.

Osborne, L.A. (2009) 'A dynamic transactional model of parent-child interactions.' In P. Reed (ed.) *Behavioural Theories and Interventions for Autism.* New York: Nova Science Publishers.

Osborne, L.A., McHugh, L., Saunders, J. and Reed, P. (2008) 'Parenting stress reduces the effectiveness of early teaching interventions for autistic spectrum conditions.' *Journal of Autism and Developmental Disorders 38*, 1092–1103.

Osborne, L.A. and Reed, P. (2008a) 'An evaluation of the role of reinforcement-based interventions in determining the effectiveness of "eclectic" approaches for teaching children with autistic spectrum disorders.' *Behavioural Development Bulletin 14*, 30–39.

Osborne, L.A. and Reed, P. (2008b) 'Parents' perceptions of communication with professionals during the diagnosis of autism.' *Autism 12*, 259–274.

Osborne, L.A. and Reed, P. (2009) 'The relationship between parental stress and behavior problems of children with autistic spectrum disorders.' *Exceptional Children 76*, 54–73.

Ryan, D. (2009) 'Inclusion is more than a place: Exploring pupil views and voice in Belfast schools through visual narrative.' *British Journal of Special Education 36*, 77–84.

Strain, P. (1983) 'Generalization of autistic children's social behavior change: Effects of developmentally integrated and segregated settings.' *Analysis and Intervention Developmental Disabilities 3*, 23–24.

United Nations Educational, Scientific and Cultural Organization (UNESCO) (1994) *The Salamanca Statement and Framework for Action on Special Needs Education*. Paris: UNESCO.

Warnock, M. (1978) *Report of the Committee of Enquiry into the Education of Handicapped Children and Young People*. London: Her Majesty's Stationery Office.

Warnock, M. (2005) *Special Educational Needs: A New Look*. London: Philosophy of Education Society of Great Britain.

INDEX